MASTER CONTENT STRATEGY

HOW TO MAXIMIZE YOUR REACH AND BOOST YOUR BOTTOM LINE EVERY TIME YOU HIT PUBLISH

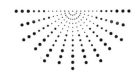

PAMELA WILSON

**BIG
BRAND
BOOKS**

©2018 BIG Brand Books
First edition

BIG Brand Books
Nashville, Tennessee, USA

PRINT EDITION
ISBN 978-0-9978754-2-3

ELECTRONIC EDITION
ISBN 978-0-9978754-3-0

Designed and produced by Pamela Wilson,
BIG Brand System

Cover illustration by D.J. Billings, aka Sparky Firepants

Edited and proofed by Paper Crane Publishing

ENDORSEMENTS

"This is the last book you need to read on how to create and share content on the internet. It has everything you need — I couldn't put it down! Every writer, blogger, podcaster, vlogger, and marketer should read it. I've been doing this kind of work for fifteen years, and I've never seen someone explain this work so clearly and so well. I already have a list of things I can do better thanks to *Master Content Strategy*." – JEFF GOINS, best-selling author of five books, including *The Art of Work* and *Real Artists Don't Starve*

"A unique and transformational approach for the frustrated content creator." – MARK SCHAEFER, author of *KNOWN*

"Pamela has penned a supremely practical guide to making sure that your content marketing strategy evolves at the precise pace your growing business does." – ANN HANDLEY, Wall Street Journal best-selling author and chief content officer at MarketingProfs

"Pamela has, yet again, served up so much value in a book, that it feels like you're taking a personalized master class in content creation success. Tactics, strategies, and tips to one side, Pamela truly knows her craft and presents all the know-how you need in a digestible and enjoyable format. Read, do likewise, and enjoy the outcome!" – CHRIS DUCKER, founder of Youpreneur.com

"In a world of content overwhelm, creative entrepreneurs need a way to stand out and be seen. Pamela Wilson's book will help you determine a strategy to create and amplify your content marketing in order to achieve your business goals. Grab your notebook and dive into this fantastically useful resource!" – JOANNA PENN, The Creative Penn

"Do you really need to read another book on content marketing? If you want practical advice from someone who's done it and provides you with not only the *what* and *why* but the *how to actually do it,* then yes, you do. You won't be disappointed with Pamela Wilson as your guide." – DAVE CHAREST, director of content marketing at Constant Contact

"WOW! No one is talking about the lifecycle approach to content strategy — I wish I would have read this right when I started my blog so I could understand that there are stages you go through. This book is a MUST for anyone who blogs at any stage — it's the *What to Expect When You're Expecting* for blogs, with a complete strategy guide on how to get your "baby" all grown up and into the world. Thank you, Pamela!" – ANDREA VAHL, co-author of *Facebook Marketing All-in-One for Dummies*

"This book manages to cover a wide range of topics, without making readers feel overwhelmed. Too many books focus on the tactics of content creation and promotion, but Pamela Wilson urges us to have a clear strategy as a foundation for success." – HENNEKE DUISTERMAAT, Enchanting Marketing

---

"A lot of people talk about strategies for content marketing that sound nice in theory and don't work out in practice. Pamela's book is the opposite — it has practical strategies that deliver results. Chapters Two and Nine can't be skipped. My recommendation is that you read this book once a year, every year until content is no longer king." – CHRIS LEMA, blogger and public speaker at Chris-Lema.com

---

"Pamela Wilson has the unique ability to not just tell you *what* to do to be effective in content marketing but also *why* and *how* to do it. *Master Content Strategy* will save you time, increase your reach, and skyrocket your results." – PAMELA SLIM, author of *Body of Work* and founder of the Main Street Learning Lab

---

"Few people understand content strategy and execution as thoroughly as Pamela Wilson. Luckily for us, she shares her wisdom in this invaluable guide to creating and using content to grow your business." – ANNE JANZER, author of *The Workplace Writer's Process* and *Subscription Marketing*

"Content isn't simply another tactic — it's the voice of strategy. This book will help you master that voice and squeeze every ounce of value from your content." – JOHN JANTSCH, author of *Duct Tape Marketing* and *The Referral Engine*

"Whether you're a writer starting your first blog or an experienced veteran managing content-rich websites, the process of creating and managing content can quickly become overwhelming. In *Master Content Strategy,* Pamela Wilson has taken the tenets of content strategy and content marketing and broken them down into action-able items and helpful checklists, making the process feel approach-able and, more importantly, achievable." – CARLA SWANK FOX, co-founder of Craft Content Nashville

---

"When I want to know what's working in content marketing, I look to Pamela Wilson. Her extensive experience has made her one of my top go-to resources I know I can trust. She always has great, new ideas about how to improve and refine strategies to create better and better results." – RAUBI MARIE PERILLI, founder and digital content strategist at Simply Stated Media

---

"I needed this book years ago. *Master Content Strategy* is not only a blueprint for creating phenomenal content for your site, but it's also a guidebook for knowing how and when to scale your strategies. Online business can be a whirlwind of chaos at times, which is exactly why you and I both need this book now." – JEFF SANDERS, keynote speaker and author of *The 5 AM Miracle*

"High-performance content marketing, the kind that builds life-time brands, requires more than "instructions." It requires years of "baked-in" experience. Pamela Wilson's *Master Content Strategy* reflects her decades of copywriting, design, and intuition-building mentoring." – ROGER C. PARKER, best-selling author of *Looking Good in Print: A Guide to Basic Design for Desktop Publishing*

"This is the most practical guide to creating your content strategy that I've ever seen. Pamela provides an easy-to-follow roadmap with checklists and templates that show you exactly what to do at various stages of your website. After reading this book, you'll be able to create and maximize the effectiveness of your content without tearing your hair out." – LISA WOOD, business coach and founder of Sprout New Media

---

"Pamela has developed an essential guide for any modern online content producer. If you care about your business, you won't want to miss this must-read book." – DAVE DELANEY, Futureforth.com

---

"This book is a complete course in modern content marketing strategy and a must-read for serious small business owners and entrepreneurs. Bonus: Pamela brings her trademark, jargon-free, and engaging writing style to breathe fun and life into a subject that may often be boring and even stodgy!" – PRERNA MALIK, conversion copywriter at Content Bistro

---

"Pamela Wilson's *Master Content Strategy* fills an unmet need in the marketplace. Wilson walks readers through the different stages of content marketing over time. She explains how to change your processes as you gain additional content marketing experience." – HEIDI COHEN, Actionable Marketing Guide

---

"I wasn't sure at first that Pamela's new book would teach me anything I didn't already know about content marketing strategy. Boy, was I wrong.

Not only have I learned useful *new* strategies I can apply in my own business but also how to better teach and train my clients on the strategies I *already* knew. The stories, examples, and analogies she uses work beautifully to help make applying them super-straightforward. A very actionable book." – JEFF BROWN, Read to Lead podcast host, coach, and mentor

CONTENTS

FOREWORD

These days, it seems like every Tom, Dick, and Harriet on the internet is starting a blog, cranking out content, and optimizing it up the wazoo for the Google gods. They're promoting it on social, begging for links, maybe even buying an ad or two for extra reach, and yet…

It's not working.

Not only is the so-called "free traffic" failing to materialize, but it seems like the few people who do read your content just don't give a damn. They don't comment, share, link, join your newsletter, buy a product, or even stay on the page for more than a minute or two. It's as if all that time and effort you're putting into content marketing is doing nothing at all.

And I have sad news for you:

It's true. If you're following the traditional approach to content marketing, it's about as powerful as farting into a hurricane. Here's why:

You're focusing on tactics when all the big wins come from choosing the right strategy. It's about doing the right things at the right time.

> *Over the last decade, I've built four different brands to over one million unique visitors per year, and the strategy I follow on Day 1 is very different from the strategy I follow on Day 1,000. The day-to-day activities evolve with the blog, and so do the required skill sets.*

What's sad is nobody tells you that. They say you need to publish a post every day, share a bunch of stuff on Facebook, and stuff in as many keywords as you can.

But that's nonsense. It's so much more nuanced than that.

The good news:

In this book, Pamela Wilson gives you a guided walk-through of those nuances, complete with strategies to follow at every stage of your journey. When you're finished reading, you'll know exactly what stage you're in and exactly what to do to get to the next stage.

If you follow her advice, you'll also get results. Not just traffic, but engagement and even sales.

How do I know that?

Because Pamela knows what she's doing. I've seen her rise from a no-name beginner to a well-known powerhouse, and that rise has been almost exclusively due to her skills as a content marketer. She understands what content to produce and when, as well as the practicalities of how to scale. Regardless of your budget or background, you're in good hands.

Just keep one thing in mind…

You still have to do the work. Research, networking, planning, writing — they're all as important as ever before.

The difference?

This time, it'll work. This time, you'll know you're headed in the right direction. This time, you'll get the results you always hoped for.

This book has what you need. So turn the freaking page, why don't ya? :-)

Jon Morrow
Founder, SmartBlogger.com
Austin, TX
August 1, 2018

YOU'RE A PUBLISHER

ON A CRISP FALL MORNING, I SAT IN AN EDITORIAL MEETING as the design department representative at a national magazine. The editor was standing his ground with a freelance writer.

"We can't publish that! Our readers will hate it!"

I sat off to the side, watching with admiration. The editor knew his audience well — what they expected when they opened the pages of the magazine. His job was to shape a compelling issue using content and images from unrelated sources. It was a little like herding cats.

Back in those days, I was focused on making the writers' words *look* great. I wanted their prose to appear compelling and easy to read, and also to be presented in a way that would make the reader want to stop what they were doing and dive into reading the magazine. I didn't shape the *content* of the magazine — I just made it look amazing once it was written.

Things have changed. Today, as the founder of BIG Brand System, a website devoted to mentoring online business owners, I've been publishing online content consistently since early 2010.

I have become a *publisher*. And if you're reading this book, *you're about to become a publisher, too.*

> *As online content creators, we are officially becoming more like magazine publishers. We're combining words and images in artful ways to draw attention and move people through our information.*

But it's not so simple as just giving ourselves a new label, is it? Let's look at what approaching content like a publisher really means.

THE CONTENT MARKETER'S DILEMMA

You may have started out writing blog posts with great enthusiasm. You had so much to say, and you now had a place to say it — and no one was stopping you from fully expressing your ideas.

That feeling usually lasts for a month or two. Then reality sinks in.

> *Creating consistent, high-quality content is tough. And the first step — deciding what to write about — can be the most difficult.*

After a short time, your blog, podcast, or video series can start to feel like a slot machine you have to keep feeding with coins (content). You pull the handle and hope the piece you just published comes up a winner.

I think that's a sad picture — don't you? We shouldn't devote our precious time and energy to something that's essentially a gamble.

Why not create your pieces and cultivate content like a magazine publisher, with a deliberate plan that will guide your efforts, exceed your audience members' expectations, and help you meet your business goals at the same time?

WHY A MAGAZINE PUBLISHER APPROACH WILL HELP YOU CREATE COMPELLING CONTENT

In this book, I'll outline how approaching your content marketing like a magazine publisher will help you create a memorable story about your business.

It's the approach I use on my own site — BIG Brand System — and it's the approach I used while managing the editorial process for one of the most-visited content marketing websites in the world, Copyblogger.

I spent two and a half years as part of the team behind Copyblogger. When I moved into the editorial department, I drew from my decades of experience putting together all sorts of publications — from magazines to books to full-color, nationally distributed newsletters.

At Copyblogger, I spearheaded a move to reinvigorate previously published posts so they could be appreciated once again. We worked with a team of designers to update the appearance of the site and make content easier to find. And I helped improve the quality of the images associated with content on the site. All with an aim to make the content easy to find, pleasant to read, and quick to absorb. This is what we'll aim to do on your website, too.

This is a book about content strategy that recognizes a few truths:

- What you publish and how often you publish it must change as your site matures.
- Consistent, in-depth content that includes multimedia elements gets more attention and engagement than content of one type (words only, audio only, video only).
- Intentionally amplifying your high-quality content will

help establish your website as a reliable resource on the web.

AN IMPORTANT NOTE FOR PODCASTERS AND VLOGGERS

Your content — whether the final format is an article, a live presentation, a podcast, or a video — usually begins as words.

Most of us work through our ideas using words, even if their final form is spoken.

Throughout this book, I'll offer you ideas for written, audio, video, and image-based content you can create to reach your prospects and customers. This book is chock-full of ideas for putting your multimedia skills to good use by repurposing content and morphing it from one media type to another.

But it almost always begins with words, so we'll focus on getting those right. You'll use words to help you structure your thoughts and plan your content no matter its final form.

Ready? Let's get started.

Pick up free bonus materials that will help you apply what you learn to your own content strategy at
MasterContentStrategy.com/bonus

PART I
INTRODUCING THE LIFECYCLE APPROACH TO CONTENT STRATEGY

1

WHAT TO EXPECT AS A CONTENT CREATOR

BACK IN THE LAST MILLENNIUM, I FOUND MYSELF EXPECTING my first child.

It was an exciting and confusing time. In the process of growing a baby, your body does all these strange things! Foods you once loved suddenly disgust you. Smells you enjoyed begin to make you queasy. And you crave weird things you've never craved before.

I was living far away from my mother and any female relatives, so I had no one to confide in. In the midst of the week-by-week upheaval, I found consolation in a book called *What to Expect When You're Expecting*.

It was chock-full of (almost) too much detail about every month of pregnancy. It gave context to the changes I was experiencing as my child grew and developed — it helped me realize they were all normal. Knowing that these strange changes were something every mother lived through helped me take the changes of pregnancy in stride. It was all part of my new reality and completely normal.

In this book, we're going to take a *What to Expect…* approach to content strategy. The more I thought about how to teach this topic, the more I realized that there's no single approach to content strategy that will work for every type of business.

Instead, it's most useful to think about content strategy as something that evolves over time, during the lifecycle of your website as it grows and develops. I'm going to approach this topic from what *you* — as a content creator — can expect as you manage your website through its stages of growth.

WHAT IS THE LIFECYCLE APPROACH TO CONTENT STRATEGY?

The need to adapt a content strategy based on the age of the website you're creating content for was driven home for me when I moved from creating content for my growing website, BIG Brand System, to managing the massive and mature content marketing resource that is Copyblogger.

Back in 2015, I was put in charge of the editorial department of the Copyblogger blog. And I quickly realized that the content strategy needed for a mature site with nearly ten years' worth of material was completely different from the content strategy needed on a younger site like mine, which was just five years old.

You're about to learn how to adapt a content strategy to the age of *your* site. As a website and a business matures, its needs change — and its content strategy should change, too.

THE THREE LIFECYCLE STAGES: A BRIEF OVERVIEW

Your approach to raising your profile using content marketing is going to morph through the years. This book will help you anticipate and plan the work you'll do in each stage of your website's growth. You'll have a clear idea of what to aim for so you can build toward the right goals with every piece of content you create.

Let's go over the three lifecycle stages here. In the upcoming chapters, we'll cover them in detail.

YOUR NEW WEBSITE: BIRTH THROUGH YEAR 1

On a brand-new website, you'll focus on populating your pages with helpful content that establishes your expertise.

Aim for:

- **A new piece every week,** so by the end of the first year, you'll have become an experienced content creator *and* filled your website's pages with content you'll link to and from for years to come.
- **Clear, consistent categories,** so people arriving on your website understand who it's for and what it offers.
- **Polished content that makes a great impression.** Aim to hone your voice and to get better with every piece you publish.

YOUR GROWING WEBSITE: YEARS 2 THROUGH 5

Your website is still new at this stage, and now you will have some flesh-and-blood audience members. You can do things like ask them to leave a response in your comments section or on social media. You can create content to help with their real-life challenges.

Aim for:

- **A new piece at least every other week,** so you can

continue to serve up useful, engaging information your audience can count on.

- **Deep-dive content that delivers in-depth information** on specific topics that help your audience and your business.
- **Multimedia content that expands your message** to other platforms. If you haven't explored repurposing your content, this will be the time to start.

YOUR MATURE SITE: YEAR 6 AND BEYOND

At this stage, you may have 300+ pieces of content on your site. It's time to put on a new hat and start to approach your content like a resource librarian!

You may continue to publish every other week — but there's more you must do. Going forward, focus on directing visitors around your site so they can easily find what they need.

Aim to:

- **Develop an updating habit.** Some of your content is quite old. If it's still being found, is it still reflecting positively on your business? Is it still relevant?
- **Get a clear view of what content is most popular** so you can link back to it *from* newer content and link forward from it *to* newer content. (This simple tip will allow older content to help newer content.)
- **Master multimedia content** and an expanded presence on outside platforms. Make it a habit to repurpose every piece of new content you create, so it's findable in other places and helps people discover your website.

It sounds like a lot of work, but remember that you're in only one growth stage at a time. Keep this book at hand to help you navigate smoothly through the stage you're in and anticipate what lies ahead.

Let's dive into what defines Very Important Content (VIC). This is what I want you to aim for as your site evolves! After that, we'll talk about what to expect as your website comes to life, begins to grow, and matures.

2

HOW TO CRAFT VERY IMPORTANT CONTENT

Let's get the obvious out of the way right now...

There's no room in this world for boring, punch-the-time-clock, blasé content.

Well, there's *room*, technically. After all, the internet is full of it!

But there's no point in spending your precious time and resources to create original content that is indistinguishable from competing content.

My friend, if you are reading this book, that is *not* what we're aiming for here.

We're aiming to help you create:

- Content that attracts the right people to your internet home
- Content that wows them when they get there
- Content that establishes your expertise, your personality, and your appeal

- Content that keeps them on the page, consuming your ideas and engaging with your brand
- Content that invites them to stay connected so they can become customers

We're aiming to create *Very Important Content* — VIC for short.

HOW TO CREATE VIC DURING YOUR ENTIRE WEBSITE LIFECYCLE

When you have Very Important Content on your website, here's what you can look forward to:

- People arrive on your pages and think, "Clearly this business knows what it's talking about."
- Your content feels human, approachable, and likable
- Your information is clear and easy to understand
- Readers, listeners, or viewers stay engaged through the entire piece of content because it has an underlying structure that makes it easy to follow

To bring VIC to life, you need to aim for *quality* content, not *quantity* content.

And this can be difficult in the early days! Your goal on a brand-new site is to fill it with content as soon as you can.

But I want you to stop, take a breath, and think BIG.

THINK BIG IMPACT

Solid content creation habits, established early and done consistently, will pay off BIG in the long run.

In a moment, we'll talk about what those habits are and how you can put them in place, whether you're just starting out or your site is already established.

Before we talk about habits, though, I want to ask you a crucial question:

What's your BIG goal?

On my own site, BIG Brand System, I often refer to this as *your BIG.*

Your BIG is the reason you're in business, and I urge you to identify this and find a way to keep it top of mind as you create your content. Your BIG can be anything that contributes meaning to your life.

For many business owners, their BIG motivation is revenue. But revenue and profits aren't the only way to measure success. The beautiful thing about owning a business is that *you* get to decide what your BIG will be!

A few options outside of the usual I-want-to-make-money goals could be:

- I want to have a BIG impact and help a lot of people with my insights
- I want to create a BIG supportive community in my niche
- I want BIG recognition within my profession
- I want BIG location and time freedoms, so I can work when I want and where I want
- I want to leave a BIG legacy with my thoughts, ideas, and points of view
- I want to have a BIG impact as I serve customers with my products or services

Before you dive into content creation habits, take a moment to decide what your ultimate goal is. Then find a way to make that goal visible! Write it on a sticky note you post nearby, put it in a small frame on your desk, write it large on a whiteboard in your space, or make it your computer desktop's wallpaper.

Keep your BIG goal in mind as you create your Very Important Content. Build habits that will support you as you work toward your BIG goal.

Let's dive into those content creation habits now.

OPTIMIZE YOUR CONTENT SO IT'S EASY TO FIND

This part is written for content creators who want to put search engine optimization best practices in place from the start. But if you're a search engine optimization (SEO) expert, jump ahead to the next section!

Optimizing for search engines from the start is a smart idea, by the way. When you optimize your content so it's easy to find, that content will bring the right people to your website for years to come.

And if you *don't* optimize your content?

Well, let's just say that, no matter how much you promote it through email and social media marketing, you'll struggle to get your content out into the world beyond your current followers or subscribers.

Search-engine-optimized content is content that anyone in the world can find. Let's get it working for you. Here's what I want you to do for each and every piece of content you create:

Find keyword phrases to target. Don't aim for single words — string together a phrase that describes what your ideal audience member would type into a search field to find your information on the topic.

This can be a tedious process. I recommend sitting down with a short list of upcoming content and doing all the keyword research in one session. Remember to note alternate phrases to see if you can weave some of those into your content as well. Search engines get smarter every year, so even if you don't use the exact combination of words searched, if you've used phrases with a similar meaning throughout, your content will be served up in their results.

Use your target keyword phrase in the headline, first paragraph, and in at least one subhead. These are important locations that will tell search engines this phrase indicates what your content is about.

Use your alternate keyword phrases throughout. Weave variations of your keyword phrase naturally into the rest of your content to give it the best chance of being found.

Link backward *before* you publish, link forward *after* you publish. As you write content on an established site, find older content that reinforces your ideas and link back to it before you make your content live. More importantly, after your new content is live, find older, established content that is already ranking for the search engines, and add links from that old content to the content you've just published.

Optimize your images. To hedge your bets with search engines, rename your image files to include your target keyword phrase before uploading them. When adding the alt description to your image — which stands in for the image if the image isn't available or images are turned off in the browser — make sure your description covers what's in the image and includes your keyword phrase as well.

Whew! That's a lot of work. But think of these steps as healthy content creation habits. The more consistently you do them over time, the better shape your content will be in for years to come.

Let's move on to the fun stuff…

CREATE HIGHLY SHAREABLE CONTENT

It's one thing to have search engines share your content. Think of them as machines that you're trying to convince to serve up your information.

> *When you're ready to take it to the next level, start trying to convince humans to share your content.*

There are a few traits you can incorporate into your content to increase the chances your human audience will want to share it with their friends and colleagues.

In-depth. Here are a few questions: If your piece of content was the only one someone would find on your topic, what would it include? What questions are your audience members wondering about, and how can you include their questions and your answers in your piece? What step-by-step process do you want them to understand, and how can you spell it out? What other media can you include — such as screenshots, additional images, or video tutorials — to make your content ultra useful? In-depth content gets shared, book-marked, and saved. Aspire to create the kind of content your site visitors want to save and share.

Easy to read. Don't turn off potential readers by serving up a monolithic wall of unbroken text. Break up your writing by:

- Chunking it down into short paragraphs of no more than three to four sentences

- Adding frequent subheads to divide your content into logical sections that are easy to skim
- Incorporating visual breaks with bulleted lists, like this one, and blockquotes (also known as *callout quotes*) like the "When you're ready…" sentence a few paragraphs back
- Adding simple formatting like **bold** and *italic*
- Adding at least one big, beautiful image to the top to draw in readers and add meaning to your words

Content that's easy to read is more likely to be consumed. And content that's consumed is more likely to be shared! Spend a few minutes polishing your content, so it looks its best before you hit publish.

Entertaining. I know — you're not in the entertainment business. Neither am I. Here's what to keep in mind — your content doesn't have to entertain an auditorium full of people. At any given moment, one single reader is absorbing your words. One single listener has your voice in their ears. One single viewer is watching your video. All you have to do is entertain that one person.

Think of your job as entertaining the single friend who's sitting across from you — just try to make them smile, engage with your examples, or relate to your story. Content that entertains gets more shares, too — people want to send fun things to their friends and colleagues because it reflects well on them.

MAKE IT LAST: BUILD FOR LONG CONSUMPTION TIMES

This goes back to the in-depth content recommendation in the previous section. Content that is well-planned, well-structured, backed with research, and yet easy to read is content people will spend time with.

And there is some evidence that when people spend time reading, listening to, or watching your content on your page, search engine algorithms interpret that as a sign of quality.

Consider incorporating elements that make your content a multi-media experience. Serving up information across learning modalities — both visual and auditory — will help make it memorable. Plus, these modalities take time to absorb and will keep visitors on your page a bit longer. Here are a few ideas:

- A slide deck uploaded to SlideShare and embedded back on your page
- A video presentation on your topic — perhaps first served up on a social media platform — that is embedded on your page, ready to be watched and enjoyed alongside the written information
- An infographic that spells out the main points in a step-by-step fashion

One or more of these elements will keep people engaged on your page and will tell search engines that your content is answering the question that drove them to the search engine in the first place.

BUILD YOUR CONTENT FOR LIST GROWTH

When you're building an online business, your time is limited. Your content needs to be part of a larger strategy to draw an audience to your website.

But it's not enough to just *bring them to your doorstep*. You need to *invite them in* and *convince them to stay a while!*

The best way to do this is to ask people to share their precious email addresses with you. And since "I need more email" is not a phrase I have *ever* heard, you're going to need to give them a compelling reason to hand over the key to their inboxes.

These days, that usually looks like some kind of instant gratification solution, otherwise known in the industry as an *opt-in incentive* or a *content upgrade*. What's the difference?

An opt-in incentive is a standard free giveaway you offer across many pages on your site. It solves a problem or provides information about your website's main topic. Use this incentive to state your philosophy and bring people into your ecosystem of beliefs, information, and approach.

A content upgrade is a quick solution to a very specific problem related to the topic of a piece of content. Read on for more ideas on what to create.

Years ago, you might have put together an in-depth video tutorial series, a 17-book content library, or a 28-day email course. But since "I need more content to read and absorb" is another phrase I have *never* heard, my recommendation is to create something that will solve an immediate problem quickly and offer it in exchange for their email address.

That may look like:

- A start-to-finish checklist for performing a vital task related to your content topic
- A single short tutorial video that shows how to solve a problem
- A template or fill-in-the-blank worksheet for writing important copy
- A short quiz that reveals useful feedback once it's submitted (feedback that you will deliver to their inbox)
- A quick buyer's guide or toolkit that's a well-researched reference list of resources in your industry

Think instant, valuable, quick wins. Once you've delivered the content upgrade, you'll want to continue to nurture subscribers with more information on the topic and even an occasional offer.

For more on content upgrades, see Chapter 15, "Content Upgrades as Email List Builders."

CHECKLIST | HOW TO CRAFT VERY IMPORTANT CONTENT

Remember, content marketing that moves you closer to your business goals is *strategic*. That means:

- Keeping your BIG goal front and center
- Looking for keyword phrases that make your content easier to find using search engines
- Aiming to wow your site visitors once they arrive on your page
- Delivering thorough, in-depth content that keeps them engaged, using multimedia to appeal to their senses
- Inviting them to stay connected by featuring either an opt-in incentive or a content upgrade that visitors will share their email addresses to get access to

I'll share more on how to get your content created in the second part of this book, Content Marketing Crash Course.

In the meantime, let's dive into content strategy! That's why we're all here, and I can't wait to share a new, easy approach with you.

Get free resources at MasterContentStrategy.com/bonus

3

YOUR NEW WEBSITE: BIRTH THROUGH YEAR 1

C ONGRATULATIONS ON YOUR BRAND-NEW WEBSITE!

Staring at a blank Posts page can make your upper lip break out in beads of sweat. You have to fill the vast, empty space with your content, and that thought can feel overwhelming.

It's a little like how I felt when I stood watching my first baby sleep. The thought washed over me, "Look at what I've done! I am now responsible for much of the growth and development that happens from here." It was an awesome responsibility — and one I didn't feel entirely ready to take on, truth be told.

Before we dive in, let's take a moment to reframe the experience and build some excitement about all the possibilities ahead.

"NOW THAT I KNOW BETTER, I DO BETTER."

The first year of creating content for a brand-new website is all about learning. Please have compassion for yourself as you master the job. Populating a pristine website with useful content is a daunting task. Take a deep breath, adopt an attitude of genuine curiosity, and ask:

What will this experience teach me?

One of my favorite quotes of all time is from Maya Angelou. I love it because it reminds us that one of the delights of this life is that we never stop learning. Here's what she said:

"I did then what I knew how to do. Now that I know better, I do better." – MAYA ANGELOU

The early days on a brand-new site will require you to make a lot of educated guesses about the content you create. *Do the best you can with what you know.* You may have very few site visitors in these early days, so at first, write to an imaginary audience of the people you hope to attract.

As people begin to flock to the information you publish, you'll know better — you'll truly understand their challenges, their fears, and their dreams. And the more you know about them, the better your content will become.

DAYDREAM TO FIND YOUR AUDIENCE

The best content feels personal and approachable. It reads like it was written *by* a human and *for* a human.

But if there are no actual humans reading what you write, how do you pull this off?

It's time to fire up your imagination, my friend. Let's get super clear on exactly the type of person you want to draw to your website. Let's be unafraid to get *very* specific — the more specific, the better.

In these early days, this will involve some daydreaming, so you can get inspired by the people you want to attract.

Have you ever arrived on a website that had the *exact* information you needed, and you had an overwhelming sense of gratitude that someone out there "got" you?

That is the sensation we want to create when your ideal audience member arrives on your pages! We want your website, your information, your writing voice, and your brand to feel like home to them. And the way to make that happen is to make some choices early on in the lifecycle of your website about who you want to appeal to.

INVITE SOME IN, LEAVE SOME OUT

I have taught marketing to non-marketers for decades. And between you and me? This next concept is one of the *most* difficult for non-marketers to embrace. But it's essential. Seriously. So please keep an open mind for what I'm about to share.

> *To create content that makes people feel like you "get" them, you have to be willing to **focus** on one group of people and **exclude** other groups.*

But it's tough to take this approach because, in the early days, you're happy for any site visitor you can get. It's hard to accept that alienating some people is a smart approach to marketing your business.

But it is. Here's why.

Content that feels personal gets that way because it has been written for a *specific person*. And especially in the early days, when real site visitors are scarce, you're going to have to create a vivid vision of the real person you want to attract. That vision will guide the topics you write about and the tone of voice you use.

Some people won't respond to your personal, specific content — and that's the point!

If you write to the wrong person, you'll attract them. Content marketing is a lot of work. If you spend weeks, months, and years creating and publishing content that draws the wrong person to your business, what's the point? The wrong person is someone who:

- Isn't passionate about the topic you write about
- Doesn't have any issues that your content and your business could solve for them
- Has those challenges to solve, but doesn't have money to spend on the solution
- Won't help to share or recommend your website because it doesn't excite them

As you can see, there's nothing inherently wrong with the "wrong" person. It's just that they lack enthusiasm around your topic. This means they won't be devoted audience members, they won't share your work, and they won't spend money with your business.

Now let's paint a different picture: What happens when your content attracts the exact right people to your website?

If you write to your ideal audience member, you'll attract the best prospects and customers for you. They'll recognize themselves in your content, become loyal to your business, and share it with friends. Your ideal audience member is someone who *needs* your content. They...

- Are passionate about the topic you write about — obsessed, even
- Currently struggle with issues that your content and your business could solve for them
- Have money to spend on solving their challenges

- Are enthusiastic fans who share or recommend your
  website because it excites them

Stop for a moment and think about what it would be like to
manage a website that draws enthusiastic audience members like
the ones described above. Take a breath in, let that breath out ...
and *feel* it.

Pretty awesome, right?

It takes *courage* to be particular about the kind of person you want
to attract. It takes *courage* to write content that you know will
alienate some people. It takes *massive courage* to reject the ideas of
creating content to attract a crowd, aiming to go viral, and pushing
to get meaningless traffic to your website.

But that's exactly what I'm asking you to do. Let's create a vivid
vision of this ideal audience member. I want them to feel so real
that you can almost imagine them sitting across from you as you
create your content.

WHY YOUR EXCLUSIVE CONTENT MAY REACH OTHERS, TOO

Here's what's fascinating about targeting your content toward a
particular person: Other people will show up, too.

Think of it like fishing. When people head out to sea, looking for a
specific type of fish, they:

- Point their boats to where that type of fish has been
  spotted before
- Put out bait they know will appeal to the kind of fish they
  want to catch
- Take a net that will hold the type of fish they're looking
  to catch

Despite all these precautions, other types of fish will swim into the net! Sometimes they're just passing through. But sometimes they decide to snack on the bait that was dropped into the water.

That's how it is when we use *targeted content*. When we're targeting our ideal audience member, we'll attract lots of people who look like them. But we'll also attract some curious "others" who want to snack on our topic, or who might aspire to be like the people we're targeting, so they hang out on the periphery.

So don't be afraid to target specifically. Other people who are truly interested will self-identify and swim right into your content net.

There's more on this in Chapter 10, "Serve Your Site Visitors with Targeted Content."

GET TO KNOW YOUR IMAGINARY AUDIENCE MEMBER

Let's dig down into this ideal audience member of yours. Answer these questions about them. Remember, if it's the early days of your website, you'll need to make educated guesses about these answers.

WHAT BIG, OBVIOUS PROBLEM DOES YOUR IDEAL AUDIENCE MEMBER KNOW THEY WANT TO SOLVE?

Let's pull back and think about what drove them to search for your information in the first place. What challenge are they looking to solve? Think of big, juicy problems like:

- How to be a better father
- How to build a sustainable e-commerce business
- How to lose weight after 40
- How to write winning grant proposals
- How to learn to swim as an adult

- How to take their hard-earned expertise and translate it into an online business they love
- How to make nutritious dinners in less than 20 minutes

What's the big problem they want to solve? What are they typing into a search engine?

WHAT PROBLEM DO YOU THINK THEY HAVE ... THAT THEY MAY NOT KNOW ABOUT YET?

You may have a lot of experience with your topic, which means you understand not just the problem but also the *cause* of the problem. What else do you think your ideal audience member struggles with? These could be hidden issues like:

- Low self-esteem
- Lack of knowledge
- Poor work ethic
- Mindset issues
- Paralyzing fears

Look below the surface of the public-facing problem. What's happening behind the scenes that may be contributing to the issue? What else does this ideal audience member struggle with?

WHAT DOES YOUR IDEAL AUDIENCE MEMBER KNOW THEY FEAR?

Your ideal audience member is aware of some of their fears. Which ones do they know for sure are holding them back? Their fears may be that:

- They don't want to look stupid
- They don't want to spend more than they can afford

- They don't want to waste time
- They don't want to hear negative feedback from friends and family
- They don't want to make the wrong move

If you asked your ideal audience member to tell you what they feared, what would they say?

WHAT ELSE IS GOING ON IN THEIR LIVES?

Our ideal audience members are juggling a lot. The more we're aware of the entirety of their lives, the more compassionate and personal we can get in our content. Give context to the content you create by answering as many of these questions as you can:

What are the demands on their time? (Remember, you may be imagining some of this!)

- They may have a 9-to-5 job
- They may work overtime or put in many working hours
- They may have babies or active young children
- They may make daily workouts a priority
- They may have a long commute

What are the demands on their money?

- They may owe student loans
- They may live month-to-month with their income
- They may consider themselves savers, or they may be spenders
- They may have to watch every dollar, or they may have some breathing room in their budget

Most "ideal customer" exercises lead with demographic questions about gender, age, education level, etc. As you can see, we're steering away from that kind of information. Instead, I'm asking you to get inside the heads, hearts, and lives of your ideal audience member. Just two more questions to go…

Where are they in their lives or careers?

- They may be just starting out in life or their career, or they may have loads of life or work experience.
- They may be happy with the trajectory of their life so far — or not
- They may love their work, or they may hate it
- They may have fulfilling family relationships — or not
- They may be looking for a solution to their high stress level

If they're searching for a solution on your site, **what's their experience level with your topic?**

- They may be starting to become aware of your topic — they're beginner audience members
- They may be trying to use your topic in their lives or careers — they're intermediate audience members
- They may be trying to function at a professional level with your topic — they're advanced audience members

It's a good idea to create content for people at different experience levels, and we'll talk about that more in the "Where Is Your Customer on Their Awareness Journey?" section of Chapter 10.

TAKE YOUR ANSWERS AND MAKE A PERSON

Take your answers to those questions and make a person from them! Imagine this person very specifically:

- What do they look like?
- What do they sound like?
- If they were sitting across from you, how would they introduce themselves?

Make this ideal audience member as tangible as you can. Then when you create content, imagine they're right there in the room with you. *Write or speak directly to them.* This is the secret to creating personable content! Write to that one specific person you want to reach. When you do, they'll recognize themselves in everything you create for them.

CONTENT GOALS FOR YOUR NEW WEBSITE

On a brand-new website, you'll focus on populating your pages with helpful content that establishes your expertise. During the first year, you want to build a strong content foundation that you'll add to in future years. Aim to publish a new piece of content every week, and have one or two pieces in reserve in case you need them.

*This means you're going to be creating a **lot** of content.*

The bad news? You're about to get *really* busy. The good news? You're about to get *really* good at creating content.

The reason you'll get good at it is that you're going to practice all the steps, over and over, week after week. If you're new to this, I highly recommend my first book *Master Content Marketing: A Simple Strategy to Cure the Blank Page Blues and Attract a Profitable Audience.* It was written with brand-new content creators in mind, and it will give you a structure and a system to follow that will support you in your early efforts.

Probably the most useful chapter in *Master Content Marketing* laid out my 4-Day Content Creation System. In Chapter 9 of the book you're holding in your hands right now, I've summarized the system so you can become familiar with it.

In this crucial first year of your new site, focus on creating one polished piece of content every single week. And choose a social network where you believe you'll find this ideal audience member you're targeting. Use this as the primary place you'll *amplify* your content (more on that in Chapter 14).

Pick an official publication day and consider it a hard deadline you *must* meet, no excuses allowed. The 4-Day Content Creation System is designed to help you easily publish weekly content, and it will show you how to set up your schedule to make it doable.

I'm going to warn you right now that life *will* intervene during this first year.

You'll get sick. Your child or spouse will get sick. You'll go on vacation. You'll immerse yourself in the work of creating a new offer, and you will have no time to spare on content creation. You'll be asked to speak at an event. Your bowling league will end up going to the national championships.

Anything could happen! So plan for it.

Not only do I want you to set up your weekly schedule using my easy 4-Day Content Creation System but I also want you to bank one or two pieces of content ahead of time. Make a "content deposit" for your site in the form of one or two finished articles, podcast episodes, or videos that you can publish when life (inevitably) throws a wrench into your plans.

One of the most important things you can do for this foundational content is to create it *strategically*. When done right, you'll link back to this first-year content for many years to come.

Your content categories are an important part of your strategy, and it's smart to set them up and use them right from the start. For more on categories, read on.

HOW TO USE CONTENT CATEGORIES DURING YOUR FIRST YEAR

Content categories are like sections of a library. When you're looking for a new book, the first thing you do is find the part of the library where that category of book is shelved.

When you apply smart categories to your content from the very beginning, you create a well-thought-out system for finding information on your website. This means that, years from now, someone arriving on your website for the first time will be able to easily find exactly what they need.

I'm kind of a categories geek — I wrote a whole chapter on the topic for *Master Content Marketing.* It puzzles me that some sites choose not to display categories. They are an efficient and easy way to direct website visitors around a content-rich site and to keep them engaged in your information. Search engines like to see that people land on a site and then stick around, so why not enable something that helps them do that?

The only compelling reason for not showing categories is if you haven't applied them consistently. Let's avoid that fate and set up your site with useful categories from the start.

The ultimate goal is to have a short list of categories — maybe 8 to 10 total — that serve as the major sections of your content library. Beyond categories, most content management systems use *tags,* which are more specific.

Think of it like this: Categories direct your site visitor to a *section* of information, like a section of a library. Tags direct your site visitor to *specific topics within that section,* like a specific bookshelf that contains books on a topic.

Let's look at some examples to reinforce how you'll use categories and tags.

A category and a tag from a website about organic gardening:

- **Category**: Flowers
- **Tag**: Zone 7 perennials

A category and a tag from a website about bodybuilding:

- **Category**: Workouts
- **Tag**: At-home workouts for beginners

A category and a tag from a website about parenting toddlers:

- **Category**: Meal ideas
- **Tag**: Breakfast recipes

If you haven't used categories or tags before, start by thinking of a short list of categories — perhaps 4 or 5. Use those for the initial content you create. If you begin to see that you'll consistently create content that fits in a different category, add a category for that content.

Keep your categories simple and clear — this is not the place to be clever! Try to put yourself in the shoes of the person arriving on your site to find the information they need. Name your categories using the words they'd use.

Tags are hyper-specific, and you can have many more of them. You still want to be thoughtful about creating new tags. Try to add new tags only when you expect to have multiple pieces of content that will include the specific topic of the tag.

USE YEAR 1 TO BUILD YOUR CONTENT CREATOR MUSCLES

The first weeks and months of creating content for a brand-new site may feel awkward and uncomfortable, especially if you don't consider yourself a born writer, podcaster, or video producer. I'm here to tell you — if you stick to this ambitious one-new-piece-of-content-each-week schedule, by the end of Year 1, you'll be a much better content creator. That weekly practice will build your content creator muscles!

It's no less of a transformation than the one a baby goes through in their first year. They're born helpless and incapable of doing much for themselves. But give them a year to develop, and most babies are walking, talking, confident *people* who have carved out a place in the world, developed a personality, and managed to enchant all those who know them.

> *That's going to be you in a year if you commit to creating a new piece of content every week!*

Aim to hone your voice and get better with every piece you publish. Polished content that makes a great first impression is a worthwhile goal, and it will benefit your business for years to come.

REPURPOSING CONTENT ON YOUR BRAND-NEW WEBSITE

First, a definition. *Content repurposing* is the practice of taking an original piece of content that exists in one form — written, audio, or video — and morphing it into a new form. Content repurposing is smart — it maximizes the impact of your ideas by offering them up in various media types and on more than one platform. This gives your content the widest possible reach.

Content repurposing is a great idea and a fantastic habit to adopt. And it may be a bit too much for you in the early days of your website! We'll talk a lot more about content repurposing in upcoming chapters.

For now, focus on getting yourself on a schedule and filling your site with high-quality, engaging content you'll be proud to call your own. You can work on content repurposing once you've made it through the first year.

MINDSET ISSUES ON A NEW SITE

If you're a first-time website owner, publishing your initial content can feel very scary. And if you don't consider yourself a "born" writer — or podcaster or video producer — it's even more intimidating. You're doing something in a very public way that you may not feel you do very well at first. If that sounds like you, I have great news —

No one is watching.

Yes, you may be lucky enough to have some friends and family members who tune in during the early days. But for the most part, your brand-new site won't have a lot of traffic. This can be frustrating, but I urge you to embrace this as an opportunity to practice in public and to refine your skills while your audience is small.

I also want to encourage you to make *sticking to a consistent publishing schedule* your primary goal at this stage. There's nothing else that will build your skills more efficiently than simply committing to practicing them on a regular basis.

You have a *lot* to look forward to! By the end of this intense first year of content creation, you'll be a stronger content creator, you'll have a site full of content, and you'll feel confident and ready to take your content to a whole new level, which is what we'll cover in the next chapters.

CHECKLIST | YOUR NEW WEBSITE: BIRTH THROUGH YEAR 1

You have a few important goals in the first year of a brand-new website:

- Make educated guesses about your ideal audience member and create content that will attract those people you'd like to work with
- Build your content creator muscles by sticking to a regular publishing schedule
- Begin establishing your core content categories and creating content to build them out

Use Year 1 to establish great habits and grow your content marketing skills. You're moving from daydreaming about your ideal audience member to serving flesh-and-blood readers, listeners, or viewers, so pay close attention to who shows up on your pages and be willing to adapt your content to meet their needs.

Your future success will build on the work you do during this crucial first year, so be prepared to show up and work intensely to get your new site off to a strong start.

4

YOUR GROWING WEBSITE: YEAR 2 THROUGH YEAR 5

YOUR WEBSITE IS STILL PRETTY NEW AT THIS STAGE, BUT IT'S very likely that something important has changed —

You now have some flesh-and-blood audience members!

The huge advantage you'll notice at this stage is that you're able to move from the abstract and imaginary to the real and concrete. This means you can create content based on the feedback, questions, and problems you notice when you interact with your site's visitors, whether that's in your comments section or on social media platforms where they respond to your content.

Here's the other change: If you've followed the recommendations in this book so far, by Year 2, you are an experienced content creator. That means you can turn your attention toward a loftier goal: increasing the *quality* and *value* of your content. That's what this chapter is about.

Quality is not an act; it is a habit. – ARISTOTLE

If I were your athletic coach and you had trained with me for a full year, I would be adding difficulty and complexity to your workout routines at this point. And I would know that you could handle it — that you *needed* it to continue to develop your skills.

That's why I want you to focus specifically on increasing the *quality* of the content you create during this stage. This is not the time to rest on your laurels and punch the content time clock.

In Year 1, you built consistency and skill. Now we're going to leverage your hard work to take your content up a notch.

THE REASONS TO INCREASE QUALITY STANDARDS FOR YEARS 2 THROUGH 5

You're not a newborn content creator anymore. Now you've grown into your own identity. You are likely feeling pretty comfortable creating content with your unique voice — that's a natural result of the large volume of content you've produced.

Now that you're coming of age as a content creator, let's set some exciting new objectives for creating content that will benefit your business. Taking your content to a new level of quality should help you:

- **Stand out from the competition** because of your in-depth, high-quality content
- **Establish your authority as a thought leader,** which can lead to speaking opportunities, podcast interview requests, and more
- **Attract a larger audience to your website** because your valuable content is being shared more often
- **Rank higher in search engines** because your content is in-depth and trustworthy

The best news of all is that the results you'll see from increasing your standards should also help the bottom line of your online business.

HOW TO CREATE IN-DEPTH CONTENT THAT PEOPLE AND SEARCH ENGINES LOVE

Quality content is in-depth content. It may be longer and contain research or quotes from thought leaders. It is definitely visually polished with formatting that increases readability, like blockquotes and bulleted lists. Oftentimes, multiple images are added to break up the page and to make the content look inviting and easy to read.

One big advantage of featuring multimedia content is that consuming it keeps people on your page longer. And when people spend more time on your page, search engines interpret it as a sign that your content is high-quality and engaging (which it *is*, if you're doing what we're talking about here). When search engines perceive your content to be of higher quality, they will rank it higher in their results, which means more site visitors for you and a growing audience for your online business.

In this stage, as you create content that helps with the real-life challenges of your new readers, listeners, or viewers, you can do it at a different pace and take your content to a deeper level. During this Growing stage of your site, aim for the goals below.

RAISE YOUR STANDARDS AND PUBLISH A PIECE OF HIGH-QUALITY CONTENT AT LEAST EVERY OTHER WEEK

Your goal in Year 1 was to lay down a solid foundation of content with a weekly publication schedule. You may have found it challenging to keep up the pace of publishing a new piece of content every single week. But if you've done so, and that content is in place, you can consider changing your publishing schedule starting in Year 2.

Because I'm going to ask you to create longer, more in-depth, and better quality content starting this year, you may find it easier to do if you dial back your publishing frequency to once every other week.

> *If publishing less frequently means you have the mental bandwidth to spend more time and effort on your content so the end product is better, go for it.*

Your overarching goal is to continue to serve up useful, engaging information your audience can count on. If you decide to do that a little less frequently, you should still set a schedule and stick to it. It's much easier to keep yourself on track if you say, "Every other Tuesday is publishing day" (or whatever day of the week you choose to publish).

You can build the rest of your content production schedule around this self-imposed deadline. And you can still use the 4-Day Content Creation System as laid out in Chapter 9. But you may add in steps for creating content upgrades, finding and adding more images, building slide decks, etc. More on all of these to come.

CREATE DEEP-DIVE CONTENT THAT SHARES IN-DEPTH INFORMATION

Now that you're getting to know your audience better, you can create content around specific topics that help your prospects, customers, and — ultimately — your business.

What is *deep-dive content*? It's content that's more in-depth than what you may have created up to now. Let's look at some qualities that great deep-dive content shares:

- **It's longer than your usual content.** Deep-dive written content may be 2,000 words or more. Or it may have fewer words but include additional media, like images, a slide deck, a video, or an audio recording. Podcasts or video content might be longer than previous episodes, feature more reference links, or offer downloadable content that complements the episode topic.
- **It incorporates a variety of media.** As mentioned, deep-dive content goes beyond the original media format, whether that's written, audio, or video. Adding information in a different format allows you to appeal to more of your audience's senses, and it will help make your information easier to remember and apply.
- **It features ample research, additional quotes, expert interviews, or case studies.** Deep-dive content shows that you have done your homework! You take the time to research your topic and include what you learn with citations. You interview thought leaders in your field, and you weave their answers into your content. You feature case studies from customers who've solved a problem around your content topic.

Focus on repurposing content to expand your reach

The deep-dive multimedia content you'll create at this stage will come together on your website — but some of it may also live on other platforms. There's more on repurposing later in this chapter and in Chapter 13 of this book.

Examples of repurposing include:

- **Additional images that break up longer content.** For long written content, break up the text every 400 to 500 words with an image that enhances what's shared in the section below it.

- **Slide decks that reinforce your main points.** Create simple slides to highlight the main teaching points in your content. Upload the slide deck to SlideShare, and embed it in your post.
- **Videos that share additional information.** Upload your video to YouTube, so it builds your presence on that platform, and embed it in your article to add to the information there.
- **Recordings that offer a portable audio experience.** Record your written article and include the audio on your page for audience members who prefer to listen or are visually impaired.

If this feels daunting, remember that if you follow the recommendation to publish every other week instead of weekly, you now have two weeks to devote to the content creation process. You'll spend more time creating this high-quality content, but you'll have more time, too.

You give yourself more time so you can take your content quality to the next level.

USE CONTENT TO BUILD YOUR EMAIL LIST

One important effort you'll make at this stage of your business is to grow your email list. And an ideal way to do this is to add *content upgrades* to your published content.

Content upgrades offer additional information that complements the blog post, podcast episode, or video you've published. To get access to the information, users have to give you their email address so you can send it to them. You must ask their permission to send them additional information beyond the content upgrade they're signing up for, but once you have that permission, you can nurture your relationship via their inbox.

Content upgrade ideas include:

- Extra tips or resources about your content topic
- A worksheet where audience members can think through how to apply your information to their own businesses
- A checklist they can use to keep track of step-by-step tasks
- A free course with additional information delivered via email, audio, or video
- A quick tutorial video showing how to apply what you've taught
- Swipe files, shared documents, or scripts that give them a head start and help them make quick progress

The question to ask yourself is, "If I were *really* into this topic and wanted to apply it in my business today, what extra information would make it easier to get started?" The answer to this question can become your content upgrade.

In Chapter 15 of this book, I share an approach to creating content upgrades that makes them easy to build and offer. For now, keep in mind that content upgrades don't have to be long and drawn out to be effective. Compact, actionable information that's quick and easy to implement wins the day!

THE CONTENT UPGRADE ADVANTAGE

As a website owner and email list builder, you'll soon see that content upgrades have two major advantages over other opt-in incentives.

Content upgrades are fast to produce. It's smart to use the same template for each content upgrade — it makes your job faster and keeps your branding consistent.

Content upgrades help to segment your subscribers. When someone shares their email address to get in-depth information on a specific topic, that tells you they have a high level of interest in that topic. In the future, if you offer a paid product or service that helps with that topic, you'll have a targeted list of people to make the offer to.

HOW TO CRAFT CONTENT THAT BUILDS YOUR AUTHORITY

At this stage of your website, you have enough foundational content to prove you know your topic well. To add to this self-created authority, it's smart to occasionally feature thought leaders in your industry to weigh in on the topics you write about.

Reaching out to subject matter experts allows you to establish a relationship with these industry leaders. And if the expert you feature decides to share your finished piece, that can dramatically increase your reach.

Ideas for crafting content that builds your authority:

- Send three to five questions by email with a friendly note about why you think they're the ideal person to talk about the topic
- Send a single question to a long list of people and publish a round-up-style article
- Ask if they'd be willing to join you on your podcast or a video interview

For all of the ideas above, be sure you:

- Provide a deadline with your query, and follow up as needed until you get a response
- Thank them for their contribution
- Link to their website from yours
- Send a link to the published piece of content, and ask if they'd share it

LISTEN UP! HOW TO TUNE IN TO YOUR AUDIENCE

As I mentioned at the beginning of this chapter, the big change in this stage of your business is that you have flesh-and-blood audience members who are reading, listening, and watching your content.

And if you can learn to listen closely to their questions, their challenges, and their confusions, you will have a never-ending source of content ideas that will inform your content strategy.

> When you listen closely, you can create content that makes people say, "I feel like you created this for me!"

There are a few reliable ways to tune in to your audience. I've used all of these at various times:

- **Read the comments on your published content.** Comments aren't as common as they used to be, but if your comments section is hopping, keep up with it to see what people are saying.
- **Check comments on your content that's shared on social media.** One reason blog comment sections aren't as busy these days is much of our content commenting happens on the social platforms where we share it. When you share a post on Facebook or a podcast episode on LinkedIn, track it to see how people are responding to it.
- **Create a private group.** As of this writing, Facebook

allows you to create private communities that are invite-only. This is a fantastic way to serve your most-loyal customers and to take the pulse of what's on their minds.

- **Host a focus group.** This one is a lot of work, but the rewards are enormous. Invite 10 to 12 people to connect with you one-on-one. Ask them all the same set of questions, one of which should be about what they are currently struggling with. Offer them the opportunity to ask a question of you at the end. If possible, record these sessions and have them transcribed so you can easily see patterns to what people are struggling with.

When you truly listen to the people you are serving, your content will be better, and so will your offers. Now that you have an audience, establish the listening habit and keep it up so you're always in touch with the needs of the people you serve.

BE STRATEGIC ABOUT PROMOTIONAL CONTENT

As you grow your online business over Years 2 through 5, you'll want to use content strategically to create revenue for your business. This means looking at your marketing plans, specifically your promotional calendar, and planning content that supports it.

Coming up, you have a full chapter on creating content around your promotions. For now, realize that an important part of your strategy at this stage of growing your business is ensuring that the content you publish is communicating the message your audience needs to hear when they're deciding whether to invest in your offers. That's *always* a goal for content marketing, but it is especially important to keep in mind before and during promotions.

YOU'RE COMING OF AGE IN YEARS 2 THROUGH 5

Years 2 through 5 are pretty exciting! You're no longer a complete newbie. You feel more comfortable sharing your knowledge publicly. You've built an audience of people who want and need your information.

Like a young child, you're standing on your own two feet and making your way through this exciting new world. Yes, you have a lot to learn. But each time you try something new, your confidence grows.

In this stage, focus on improving:

- **Content quality** by creating more in-depth pieces that people and search engines love
- **Your use of multimedia** by exploring things like video, audio, slides, transcripts — anything that will move your content from its original format to a different one
- **Connections with thought leaders** who can enrich your content, shine some of their authority on you, and help you get your site in front of their audiences
- **Promotional content** that meets objections your prospective buyers may have

If needed, you can decrease your publishing frequency so you can pour more time and effort into creating this high-quality content.

REPURPOSING CONTENT DURING YEARS 2 THROUGH 5

Content repurposing refers to presenting your content information in more than one media type: written, audio, video, slides, etc. Repurposing gives you a way to feature more than one content format so you engage your audience's various senses. It also makes it easy to spread your content on other platforms, extending its reach.

In the previous chapter, I recommended that brand-new site owners not worry too much about content repurposing. Now that your site is established, content repurposing should become part of your normal content process. Chapter 13 is devoted to the topic so you can learn exactly how it works.

Your goal during these years is to make content repurposing a habitual part of your content creation routine. For every piece of high-quality content you create, think about how you can extend the original message with supplementary content that:

- **Uses a different media type than the original,** so text becomes audio, video becomes text, etc.
- **Gives people a way to connect with you on a more intimate level.** Video and audio are great for this.
- **Is highly shareable on other platforms.** Additional images and video can live within your content, and they can also serve as mini-advertisements for your content when they're placed on social media sites.

This is a time to ramp up your creativity and approach your content as a sensory event that appeals to your audience members' intellects, eyes, ears, and hearts.

MINDSET ISSUES DURING YEARS 2 THROUGH 5

If this all seems like a lot of work, it is. That's why I suggested you can move to an every-other-week publishing schedule after gaining experience as a content creator through weekly publishing for the first year.

You can devote the extra time to developing higher-quality content

— the extra effort is worth it! Content created during these years builds authority and establishes you and your business as a leader in your industry. When you repurpose your content into more than one media type, it helps extend your reach on other platforms. And when you consistently create content upgrades that offer your audience a way to opt in for more information, your email list will grow — which should help your business grow as well.

And can I just say? This approach to content is a lot of fun! It's a creative challenge to step back from each piece of content and ask yourself, "How can I make this *amazing?*" The ways in which you answer that question will become a rich source of ideas that help you build your content creation abilities during these still-early years.

CHECKLIST | YOUR GROWING WEBSITE: YEAR 2 THROUGH YEAR 5

You'll come into your own as a content creator during these important growth years. This is a time when you establish habits and build on them so you step into your role as a powerful content creator who people pay attention to.

- Focus on crafting high-quality content — even if that means publishing less often. Make your content longer and more detailed. Support your main points with data, if needed. Include multimedia elements to help keep people on your page.
- Build content upgrades that complement the information you share and also grow your email list
- Build authority by occasionally publishing content with direct quotes from thought leaders in your industry
- Listen intently to the audience that you're building, so you can adapt your content topics to their needs

- Practice weaving in promotional content, so you can use your platform to keep the marketing engine of your business running smoothly
- Repurpose the content you create into different types of media that you feature on platforms outside your website

Remember, the core difference between this growth stage and the first year of your site is that you now have real prospects and customers. Tune in to their comments — both on and off your site — so you know what's on their minds and can create high-quality content and solutions that help them meet their challenges.

5

YOUR MATURE WEBSITE: YEAR 6 AND BEYOND

As your child grows, your job as a parent changes from providing sustenance for their every need to becoming more of a consultant in their lives. It moves from a hands-on role to a hands-off role.

However, on a mature site — one that is six years old or older — you have two new and important jobs. The big reason? As you enter this stage, you may have 300 or more pieces of content on your website!

> *It's time to put on a couple of new hats. You're going to approach your content like a resource librarian and a maintenance person — while still working as a content creator.*

You may continue to publish new content every other week — but there's more you must do at this stage to better serve your website visitors. Going forward, you'll focus on directing visitors around your site so they can easily find what they need when they arrive on your pages.

You're a bit of a maintenance person, as well. Older content will need updating and improving on a regular basis. You'll want to monitor the health of your older content by checking how it ranks on search engines. You now have a website that's solidly built with helpful content, and you need to keep that content in tip-top shape so it continues to work for you.

> *Basically, our goal is to organize the world's information and to make it universally accessible and useful.* – LARRY PAGE, CO-FOUNDER OF GOOGLE

We've already covered your content creator role. So what's involved in becoming your website's resource librarian and maintenance person? That's what this chapter is about.

At this stage, you'll continue to publish on a regular basis. Every other week is a minimum. As you continue with your regular publishing schedule on your mature site, you'll notice you have two advantages you didn't have before.

First, you have more than six years of experience as a content creator under your belt. Planning and creating content should feel quite natural at this point. Second, you should have a nice-sized audience of readers, listeners, or viewers. Your content will be stronger because you know it's serving real people with real challenges.

Along with creating new content, you'll also spend some of your time organizing and updating the content you've already created.

You want to keep your site updated and fresh, so it passes Larry Page's "useful" test, as mentioned above. You now have two ways to do this:

- Publish new content that answers questions, shares valuable information, and helps your ideal customer

- Update older content with new information and media assets

In this chapter, we'll look at both of these *content freshness* techniques. Because we've already spent time on how to create Very Important Content in Chapter 2, we'll focus our attention on how you can update older content with new information and assets.

ORGANIZE YOUR CONTENT TO ADD VALUE AND KEEP SITE VISITORS ON YOUR PAGES

Imagine this: You've just stepped inside one of the most renowned libraries in the world. There are three floors of books, and the stacks go back as far as your eye can see. You sense that the knowledge of the world is all around you — you can smell the paper and ink, and you can't wait to find the exact books you need.

You move quickly to the Information Desk, where you ask the librarian where you can access the online card catalogue. She looks at you with benign patience, smiles sweetly, and says, "Oh, we don't use a catalogue here. We just put the books on the shelves so you can explore them at leisure. Enjoy!"

Your heart sinks. You know that the information you need is here … somewhere. But you also know that, although you may spend hours searching, there's an excellent chance you'll never find what you're looking for.

This, my friend, may be what your site visitors feel when they land on your mature site. They sense that you have a massive amount of information to share, but — unless you've organized it like we'll talk about in the next section — they may feel the job of finding what they need is entirely up to them.

Worst of all? They may give up before they've started their search.

Let's cover a few ways you can organize your content so visitors to your mature site can find what they need quickly and easily.

CONTENT CATEGORIES

Easy-to-find information begins when you carefully add categories as you create new content, as we talked about in Chapter 3.

When you apply categories to your content, your content management system displays them above or below your content, and it makes the category names into clickable links. When someone clicks on those links, they'll be taken to a page which displays all the content on your site that has been assigned to that category.

The next technique depends on your carefully added categories to display information in a navigation menu.

NAVIGATION MENUS

Fast Company is a magazine and a website with content that dates back to 1995. Now *that's* a mature site! At the time of this writing, they are using a very slick solution to guide their site visitors toward the information they're interested in. Under the main logo at the top of the site, there is a slim, bright-yellow navigation bar with six major categories: Technology, Leadership, Entertainment, Ideas, Video, News.

When you click on one of those navigation menu items, you're taken to a category page which features a dynamic layout showcasing the most recent content in that category.

The website navigation is functioning as a resource librarian who is asking a library visitor about their main area of interest, then sending them to the section that contains all the books on the topic they want to learn more about.

If you don't want to make an entire navigation menu about your site's content, consider having a *Resources* menu item that reveals a submenu with your site's main categories. When a visitor chooses a category, serve up a page with the most recent content for that category.

HOW TO LINK TO CONTENT WITHIN YOUR WEBSITE PAGES

If your website content page features a sidebar — a long, narrow column that runs vertically alongside your content — this can be a perfect space to feature other site content. You can do this very simply with a list of links to your main category pages. Or you can create attention-getting images that, when clicked, lead to your main category pages.

Similar to your sidebar, your footer area runs along the bottom of every content page of your site. In this consistent space, you can create a list of text links that lead to the main category pages on your site.

Of course, don't forget the obvious: Be sure to display relevant categories above or below your published content. If someone is drawn to content about a specific topic, the chances are good that they'll want to consume more content on the same topic. Make it easy to find by displaying the content's category in a prominent location.

HOW TO QUICKLY PERFORM REGULAR MAINTENANCE ON EXISTING CONTENT

Your website is fully grown and mature. And as someone who is fully grown and somewhat mature, I can tell you that, at this stage of life, regular maintenance becomes more important than ever.

On a personal level, eating healthy foods, getting enough fresh air and exercise, and giving your body a good night's rest can make a huge difference in how well you function on a day-to-day basis. When you're younger, these things don't matter as much. When you're older, you *need them* in order to feel good.

Let's transfer this concept to your site: How will you keep your content in tip-top shape? How can you refresh older content so it continues to be useful? Which content is worth building up and which content can be ignored?

Just like you might make a regular appointment at the dentist to keep your teeth in great shape, block off time once every quarter to review your content results, so you can highlight content that your audience has responded to and that is helping you reach your business goals.

PINPOINT YOUR PURPOSE

In the early days of my website, BIG Brand System, my content was created for people who I affectionately call *DIY Marketers*. These are people who need to market their business themselves, for a variety of reasons, or who simply want to expand their understanding of marketing and design techniques and how to use them.

Over the years, my focus has changed to helping people with professional expertise who want to build an online business that gives their message greater reach and creates revenue at the same time.

This may happen to you, too. You may start your business with one focus and, as the years go by, your focus shifts. Your content will shift along with your focus, and you'll have categories of content you *don't* want to emphasize for fear of confusing your audience about what you deliver.

You will think about your current business focus, then look at your analytics data and eliminate any old content that doesn't support your current business goals. More on that in the next section.

LOOK AT YOUR DATA

Before you start updating content, get a clear view of what people are already finding on your site. To get that clear view of which content is ranking for you, start with your analytics software.

Most content creators I know rely on Google Analytics. If you do, too, here's how to find which content is doing well so you can turn your attention there first.

Log in to Google Analytics. In the left column, select Behavior. Under that, choose Site Content. And under that, choose All Pages. Following this sequence will tell Google Analytics to serve up a list of your most-visited pages. This is gold! Consider downloading the list and saving it on a spreadsheet, in software like Evernote, or even printed on paper.

If you have older content that is ranking well on search engines but reflects your old focus, consider updating it to bring it in line with your new offerings. Respect the existing information, but bring in how it fits within the context of your new focus.

To my dismay, my older design-oriented content was still getting lots of views as I began pivoting my focus toward online business builders. If you notice the same thing — that the content people are finding doesn't reflect your current focus — use this as motivation to make sure all your content that *does* fit your current area of focus is top quality and optimized for search engines so it will be found, too.

YOUR MAINTENANCE TASKS, IN ORDER OF IMPORTANCE

Let's spiff up your older content that's on target, in terms of your topic, and already ranking well. We want search engines — and through searches, your intended audience — to find this information, so here's what to update:

Make your headline fascinating and clickable. If the old headline leaves something to be desired, consider writing a new one. If you don't want to change the headline — maybe because you're using it in social media campaigns, you've linked to it using the headline text, or you've created graphics that feature the headline — there's an alternative.

Instead of changing the title text that displays the headline at the top of the content page, consider changing the SEO title. This is easy to do if your site uses an SEO plugin which gives you access to that title text. When you do this, the on-page headline will remain the same, but the search result headline will be updated. You can "sell" your content a little harder with the search engine headline, resulting in more clicks.

Add links to new resources. As time goes on, you may have created newer content on the same topic. Be sure you link forward from your older content to the newer information. If the older content ranks well, doing this will help boost the ranking of the newer content while giving your website visitors an easy way to find everything you've written on that topic. Be sure to link out to other high-ranking sites that can serve as a resource on the topic, too.

Include new information. As time goes on, your understanding of a topic may deepen. You may learn new approaches. Or the accepted approach to your topic may have changed. If so, be sure to update your older content to reflect current realities. Search engines like to see new information, and updating older content will signal to them that the page is fresh.

Consider republishing your content. If you completely overhaul your content, consider republishing it with a current date. You can simply add a note like this one to the bottom: *This content was originally published on June 28, 2018, and has been updated with new information and resources.*

ADD MULTIMEDIA TO CLASSIC CONTENT TO GIVE IT NEW LIFE

We've just covered how to maintain and update older content. Beyond that, think about how to go back to old content that is ranking well and supercharge it with new types of media.

During the first year of your website, I encouraged you to focus on becoming a confident, consistent content creator. I encouraged you to add multimedia to your content starting in Year 2. This means you may have classic content that performs well but needs a little extra love to make it stand out.

I have written a full chapter on this concept, which you'll find in the Supercharge Your Content Impact part of this book, in Chapter 13. The main thing to remember here is that you want to repurpose your information so it morphs into a different type of media. That means, for example:

- Blog posts become slide decks
- Podcast episodes turn into videos
- Videos become downloadable checklists
- Podcasts and videos get transcribed and become blog posts

As a mature site owner, repurposing your content is a new frontier you should explore and get comfortable doing.

FLEX YOUR CONTENT CREATOR MUSCLES ON YOUR MATURE SITE

At this point in the lifecycle of your website, I want to encourage you to flex your content creator muscles! You may not recognize it, but years of content creation have built a skill set that you can use to promote your online business.

Think of it like this: In the early days of your website, your content was being created by a newbie. Now your content is being created by a veteran, experienced, confident content creator.

Stand tall and wield those content creator chops, my friend. Look at every piece of content you create as an opportunity to wow your site visitors with the best piece of content they'll ever find on that topic.

Why worry about the competition at this point? During this stage, focus on setting high standards and improving your content quality with every passing year.

BEYOND MAINTENANCE: BE A GOOD CITIZEN AND HELP OTHERS

Remember the very early days of your new website? You didn't have an audience. You didn't have a network. You felt like you were operating in a vacuum.

Today, you're an old pro. And as an experienced content creator, I want you to think about how you'll extend your help and experience to those who are just starting out.

As new content creators reach out and ask you to participate in round-up posts, to be a guest on their new podcast, or to spend 15 minutes as an interview guest on their new video series, find a way to say Yes to as many as possible. You don't know how new content creators may grow over the years — today's newbie might be tomorrow's powerhouse thought leader in the industry! So, within reason, find a way to help those who are just starting out.

CHECKLIST | YOUR MATURE WEBSITE: YEAR 6 AND BEYOND

At this growth stage, your role will change yet again. You will continue to create content — more easily now because you have a lot of practice! But because you've developed a large body of content, you will take on the roles of guide to and caretaker of the content you've created.

- Continue publishing Very Important Content every two weeks, and now add organization and quarterly maintenance to your regular tasks
- Use your content categories to display collections of content in a navigation menu, a sidebar, or within your site's footer
- Clarify the current purpose of your site and consider changing the focus of older pieces if they don't reflect your current direction
- Use site analytics data to pinpoint popular pieces for maintenance and repurposing
- Maintain and update existing content with improved headlines, better (and more) images, new information, and updated approaches
- Consider repurposing the ideas in different formats: slide decks, video, checklists, etc.
- Extend a hand to those starting out — become a thought leader by leading

In this part, we've covered the idea of approaching your content strategy with the website lifecycle as the guide to what you'll work on.

But in the back of your mind, you might have a question looming: "How exactly am I going to get all this done?"

That's what the next part of this book is all about, so keep going. We're about to move quickly through a content marketing crash course, where we'll focus on getting content created on a regular schedule so publishing becomes the most natural habit in the world.

PART II
CONTENT MARKETING CRASH COURSE

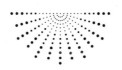

6

CREATE CONTENT THAT MULTITASKS WITH WORDS, IMAGES, AUDIO, AND VIDEO

IN THE EARLY DAYS OF CONTENT MARKETING, WE HAD WORDS. Lots of words.

Words are economical to create and easy to consume. Most anyone can type on a keyboard, and words don't take a lot of bandwidth to deliver.

That's why the earliest blogs looked a lot like pages from a book. They had no visual content to liven up the words, and no video or audio to complement the written information.

Even now, written content is the easiest format for search engines to index. They scan your words, looking for keyword phrases and meaning so they can help searchers find your information.

For pure information density per second, written content can't be beat — it should always be a core part of your content marketing mix.

But right on the heels of written content are a variety of newer formats that bring information to life on your pages. These formats communicate in a way that engages more of our senses. They keep us engrossed for longer stretches of time.

And what makes it all possible is *bandwidth.*

As faster internet speeds and sophisticated mobile devices spread across the world, visual and audio formats became not just a viable option for our content — they became a necessity.

> *The internet is now full-on multimedia. And that's great news for content creators. This is what it means to be a publisher in the digital age!*

Now, a webpage that's a wall of unbroken text looks dull and uninviting to our eyes. Websites that never offer audio or video content feel comatose. And businesses that aren't present on at least one of the highly visual social platforms — like Facebook, Instagram, YouTube, or Pinterest — are missing out on a huge opportunity.

Images are processed in a different part of our brains than words. This visual processing part of our brain isn't as busy as the verbal processing part — and it's *fast.*

It's smart to think about how to weave other types of content together to create an end product that fully engages your audience members' brains.

Plus, watching a video or listening to audio keeps visitors on the page longer — an important sign to search engines that your site visitors are engaged and your content is high-quality.

Maybe you're just beginning to master the writing process, so the thought of creating multimedia feels incredibly daunting right now. Don't worry — in the coming chapters, we're going to review my method for chunking down the content creation process into small, daily, manageable chunks.

Once you've mastered this approach, content creation will happen with natural ease. And you'll find yourself with enough time to think beyond a single format for communicating your ideas.

7

A SIMPLE WAY TO GIVE BIRTH TO YOUR BEST WORK

As you read through the "lazy" method I'll introduce in this chapter and detail in Chapter 9, remember this:

> *Whether it's written, audio, video, or image-based content, it will be most effective if there's some kind of underlying structure to the information.*

And that's really all the "lazy" method is!

You approach your content as a structure you build day by day and piece by piece. You work on different parts of the structure over several days so you never feel overwhelmed — because you've made the project smaller and more manageable. You also give your mind time to think deeply about what you want to communicate and how you want to talk about it. This guarantees richer, more thorough content.

> *Never again will you have to create content in one bleary-eyed*

marathon session — you'll work on it a little bit at a time, revisiting it and making it better with each pass.

Working this way allows your best creative work to emerge. And it allows you, the content creator, to approach your work with joy! How can content marketing become a fun part of your workday?

- **Think about your content as a body of work.** Don't put too much pressure on any one piece of content.
- **Focus on what your content will do for your business.** Remember, this happens over time, piece by piece. Patience!
- **Set yourself up for success in your physical environment.** Block out time on several days of the week to work on content in the place you work best.

You'll keep your eyes on your BIG goals when you approach your content marketing as a body of work. Read on for how to make this happen.

———

Pick up free bonus materials to create your content strategy at MasterContentStrategy.com/bonus

8

THE BODY OF WORK APPROACH TO CONTENT CREATION

IN MY BOOK *MASTER CONTENT MARKETING*, I USED PABLO Picasso as an example. I have enjoyed Picasso's body of work for decades, and I try to see it in person when I can.

Picasso was a prolific artist — he created around 50,000 paintings, sculptures, prints, and drawings in his lifetime. But many years ago, I realized something important about his work.

I have seen enough of it to realize that not every piece he created was a masterpiece — far from it. Many of his works look more like failed experiments. Oftentimes you can see him trying to express something and not quite achieving it — but then the same idea shows up in a later piece in its fully developed form.

> *I believe that this approach — using your work to develop ideas and making it your goal to create consistently — is one of the main reasons we know Picasso's name and his work today.*

History tells us that Picasso treated the people he loved with equal parts admiration and abandonment — but he never abandoned his ideas. I believe that we would do well to approach our content creation the same way.

Don't put too much importance on any single piece of content. Instead, see your content as a body of work that — as a whole — supports your business. No one piece needs to carry the full burden, and every piece you create will help you make the next piece even better.

> *When you approach content marketing like it's a creative act, it can become something you look forward to.*

Content marketing doesn't have to feel stressful. If "approach content marketing like it's a creative act" sounds daunting, read on.

HOW CREATIVE PEOPLE CULTIVATE THEIR BEST WORK

Creative people work in a very specific way. Most creative acts involve recognizable steps:

- Warming up your creative brain
- Getting initial ideas recorded
- Choosing one idea to pursue
- Doing the work to develop your idea
- Polishing the work through careful editing
- Putting the work out into the world

Important: You do *not* need to create polished work in the first sitting! Your creative work will be richer and more thoughtful if you let it develop naturally over several days.

Approaching your content marketing work in phases will take the pressure off. You can allow yourself the time and space to do great work in a stress-free environment. Let's talk about that environment next, because spending some time setting up an environment that suits you is crucial.

YOUR CONTENT CREATION STATION

Your content is created in a place and at a time. When you set up your environment so it supports you, you'll get more done, and the process will feel easier.

Your content creation station includes things like:

- **The chair you sit in or the desk you stand at.** Are they supportive and comfortable?
- **The lighting.** Would you rather work with abundant natural light, or do you prefer to work in a darkened environment, focused only on the light from your laptop?
- **The sound environment.** Do you prefer complete silence or sound in the background?
- **Your tools.** Is everything you need close at hand? This may include a dictionary, a thesaurus, a microphone, or headphones, and any other items you'd like to have close by, like a beverage, pen and paper, etc.
- **The time of day when you find content creation easiest.** Are you a morning person or a night person? Consider the time of day when creative work feels most natural to you, and block out some time to get your content created.

We'll talk about my 4-Day Content Creation System in the next chapter. Before you put the system into practice, review this chapter and set up your environment — and your mindset — for content creation success.

CHECKLIST | THE BODY OF WORK APPROACH TO CONTENT CREATION

Like any creative product, content develops best when it's given the right environment and a combination of time and space to grow into what it's meant to be.

- Approach content creation as a series of small tasks
- Don't put too much pressure to perform on a single piece of content — remember you are building a body of work, not a single masterpiece
- Become aware of the way your environment makes content creation easier or more difficult, and set yourself up to create content when and where you feel most supported

This chapter emphasizes the *creator* part of the *content creator* label. Use the methods found here to support your process and get the best possible results from the time you spend working on your content.

9

THE 4-DAY CONTENT CREATION SYSTEM OR A "LAZY" METHOD FOR CREATING CONTENT

For many of us, creating content to attract an audience is a chore we have to layer on top of the important day-to-day tasks we do to keep our businesses afloat.

Adding "write a blog post" or "record a video" to our already long to-do list can make us feel overwhelmed. And resentful.

> *Creating content with an I-have-no-choice-but-to-do-this attitude will lead you to publish uninspired, dutiful content that doesn't actually work — what a waste of your time and energy!*

Here's the thing: Creating a piece of content is not a single task. It's more like a project — a group of tasks you perform to get a big result.

In this chapter, we'll look at how creative people get big results by breaking their projects into small, doable tasks.

When you spread out the content creation process over several days, it never feels overwhelming. And you set yourself up to do your best quality work. This 4-Day Content Creation System is the same one I talk about in detail in my book, *Master Content Marketing.* I'll give you a quick overview here.

DAY 1: WRITE YOUR HEADLINE AND SUBHEADS

On the first day, you're going to set up the backbone of your content by mapping out your headline and subheads for the content you're going to create. For video, audio, or image-based content, you'll still create a headline, but the subheads will simply be the main points you want to make.

> *Truth be told, what we are doing here is creating an outline for your content.*

But let's not call it an outline! That brings back traumatic memories from English class, doesn't it?

So we'll stick with *backbone.* You're going to create a backbone that you will hang the rest of your content on.

YOUR HEADLINE

Your headline serves as a miniature advertisement for your piece of content wherever it's shared: on social media, on other websites, in your email marketing, and more. This mini-ad needs to work hard to drive people to click on the link and consume it once they arrive.

> *Your headline is what makes clicks happen. It drives people to your content. It's your 24/7 salesperson.*

Spend plenty of time writing headlines until you find one that truly sells your content. I usually recommend that people write at least 25 headline ideas before deciding which one to use. The first 10 to

15 headlines will probably be clichés or just plain boring. When it comes to headlines, don't be clever — be clear.

Remember, the best headlines make a big promise in a clear, original way. It's more important to show how people will benefit from consuming your content than to try to impress them with alliteration, wordplay, or obscure references.

YOUR SUBHEADS

Subheads are those section headlines that sit above any place in your content where you are introducing a new idea and plan to expound on it. Subheads are tricky, and here's why: You can't write your subheads until you know what your content is going to be about.

See what we're doing here? By asking you to write your subheads, I am *requiring you* to think about how you will present the information in your content.

> *This planning will make your content better because you're taking the time to think through how you'll structure your information and present it in a compelling fashion.*

You need to think about how you will take people from:

- **Point A,** where they are when they first arrive on your page, to...
- **Point B,** what you want them to understand by the time they finish consuming your content

When mapping out your subheads, aim to use three to five — or more, if you're creating very lengthy content.

WHAT DO SUBHEADS LOOK LIKE IN AUDIO, VIDEO, AND IMAGE-BASED CONTENT?

In *audio content*, like a podcast, a subhead is the place in the audio where the subject turns a corner and heads in a different direction. This new section often starts with a one-sentence introduction, a question, a short musical interlude, or a consistent phrase.

In *video content,* a subhead might include a splash screen that serves as a visual divider between the content before and what comes after.

And in *image-based content*, like a slide deck or an infographic, a subhead might look like a title slide or a new graphic style that visually introduces the new section.

> *Once you're done with these two steps, you have completed your Day 1 tasks.*

Congratulations! Take a break, walk away, and let your mind continue to work on your content as you go about the rest of your day.

DAY 2: WRITE YOUR MAIN COPY

Day 2 is all about getting a first draft finished. Once your first draft is written, you have the raw material needed to shape a beautiful, clear, polished piece of content, whether the final product will be an article, a podcast episode, or a video.

> *Until you have the raw material created, your new piece of content is just a dream.*

That's why you must focus your Day 2 work on the singular task of getting a first draft completed.

It will be messy. It will be full of typos. It will be meandering, confusing, and unclear — *that's all fine.* Your only goal is that, by the end of Day 2, your first draft needs to be *done.*

Aim for speed on Day 2. Just get your first draft written as quickly as possible.

You will have plenty of time to whip your first draft into publishable shape in your next work session. You will use Day 3 for polishing, editing, proofreading, formatting, and finding an image for your content.

How do you get this first draft of your main copy written as quickly as possible?

I recommend you set a timer. Working against a timer adds an element of gamification to your writing process that — surprisingly — can be a lot of fun. The timer on your phone or a simple kitchen timer will both work fine.

Set your timer for ten minutes, to start. Get as much written as you possibly can in those ten minutes.

Getting started is the most difficult part. Once you get started, you'll probably find that you want to continue writing. Use the timer to get over the initial resistance, and then keep going until you're done.

Focus your Day 2 efforts on getting your first draft written from start to finish, then walk away.

Take a break and prepare yourself for the work you'll do on Day 3 — polishing your content and getting it ready to publish.

DAY 3: POLISH AND PREPARE TO PUBLISH

POLISHING

Now that you have walked away from your content for a while, it will be easier to proofread and edit.

Taking a break from your content allows your eyes to "reboot" so you notice its problems and weaknesses. You may see that one section is unclear. You may realize that an argument is unconvincing and needs to be reinforced with data. You may read your first draft and decide it's incredibly dry, and it needs a story or some inspirational quotes.

Whatever the issue is, it will be easier to notice when you've taken a break from your piece of content.

At the beginning of your Day 3 work session, read through your content — out loud and in a monotone voice (do your best robot imitation). This trick helps to highlight areas that are unclear.

Once your piece is edited, it's time to give it a proofreading pass. Software like Microsoft Word or Grammarly will highlight spelling and grammar issues for you.

Remember: You are allowed to use your best judgment when it comes to correcting your mistakes. Sometimes these programs don't understand your intent. And sometimes, in the name of interesting content, you have to break a few of the traditional rules.

PREPARING

Your raw material is now ready to move into its final, prepared state.

- If you're creating a blog post, you'll format the text and add images, plus any supplementary materials like video, audio, or additional image-based content.

- If you're producing audio, you'll record and incorporate introductions, ads, and musical transitions.
- If you're creating a video, you'll film, edit, and add any splash screens and screencast recordings.
- If you're polishing a piece of image-based content, ensure that any text elements are readable and that your images are communicating what you want them to say. If you're not sure, have someone else take a look and give you feedback.

Your goal with this final formatting pass is to have an end product that *communicates*. That's what content marketing is about!

Special effects, fancy fonts, cool music, or stunning splash screen graphics are all icing on the cake (which is your useful content). Focus on getting the cake right, because no amount of delicious icing will help a cake that's inedible.

DAY 4: PUBLISH AND PROMOTE

Your content is now ready for publication. You have set it up to be released at a specific time. If you have an email list, you may send them a message to let them know that you have new content ready for them to read, listen to, or watch.

In order to drive the maximum number of people to your new piece of content, make sure you set up posts on the social media platforms you use most.

Don't be afraid to repeat yourself on social media. Let people know several times on the day of publication that you have a new piece of content for them to take a look at.

Over the next few days, continue to invite people to consume your new content.

As the weeks go on, keep this content in rotation on your social media platforms. Continue to mention it, even if it's just once a week.

When you create a particularly good piece of content, muster up the courage to reach out to other website owners and let them know about the new resource that's available on your site. You won't want to do this for every post, but when you write something that is particularly in-depth, well-researched, or a solid resource their audience might benefit from, let them know it's available so they can share it. Website owners are always looking for sources of high-quality content to share with their audiences.

CHECKLIST | THE 4-DAY CONTENT CREATION SYSTEM OR A "LAZY" METHOD FOR CREATING CONTENT

Break up the content creation process over several days. You'll give yourself a chance to see the content more than once, and with fresh eyes that are able to spot holes, confusing areas, or anything that's unclear.

- Day 1: Write your headline and subheads
- Day 2: Write your main copy
- Day 3: Polish and prepare to publish
- Day 4: Publish and promote

Now you know how to create content over time in a way that supports you doing your best work consistently.

But what should you write about to meet the needs of everyone who comes to your website? The answer to that question is just a few pages away in the next chapter.

10

SERVE YOUR SITE VISITORS WITH TARGETED CONTENT

YOU LAUNCH YOUR WEBSITE WITH ALL SORTS OF IDEAS FOR content you want to create. But eventually, your "idea well" runs dry, and that initial enthusiasm about creating your content wears off. Your "I must churn out content" voice kicks in. And you start writing, recording, and filming, almost without thinking.

On the one hand, this is wonderful — the more often you create content, the better you become.

And the more consistently you publish the content you create, the more search engines will reward your site by listing it higher in their results. They'll send more people your way, and you'll have more of an audience and future customers.

But once people arrive on the pages of your site, will they engage with the content they find? Will they see clear information that meets their current needs?

Don't just churn out random content. Approach this task with a plan to help people, no matter where they are among the levels of awareness about your topic.

Their questions are what brought them to a search engine. And if you've optimized your content with targeted keyword phrases, their questions will lead them to your content. Let's make sure your content serves up the answers they need right now.

WHERE IS YOUR CUSTOMER ON THEIR AWARENESS JOURNEY?

In my book, *Master Content Marketing,* I share a very simple way to think about your audience's needs. It's not a content strategy. It's a way to think about how to meet the expectations that drive people to the pages of your website.

One note: I talk about *readers* in this chapter, but if you create audio or video content, please swap in *listeners* or *viewers.*

Your readers will land on your site with different levels of awareness about the topic you cover. They have questions — lots of questions! But those questions will differ depending on their previous exposure to your topic.

If we were to use broad descriptions of their levels of awareness, your audience members are at a **Beginner,** an **Intermediate,** or an **Advanced** level.

> *Their awareness corresponds to a readiness to do business with you.*

Let's take a look at what each awareness level is looking for and how you can serve them.

BEGINNER READERS ASK, "WHAT IS [___]?"

Beginners might not be ready to become customers — but you need to create content for them because Beginners eventually become Intermediate and Advanced readers who are ready to invest in the topic you talk about.

Beginners have embarrassing questions. At least, that's how they feel about their questions, which is why they're on the internet, searching for answers anonymously instead of calling a friend or colleague to ask their question.

Beginners are looking for *definitions* — they want to understand your topic and clarify any jargon that's confusing. They want to make sense of concepts that are new to them.

Beginner readers are taking an early interest in your topic — often-times because life has presented them with a challenge.

> *It's important to serve Beginner readers well. They are an abundant source of new prospects for your business, and they are hungry for knowledge.*

If you deliver what Beginner readers need when they're in the early stages of their journey, they will become devoted members of your audience.

And the biggest plus is that *your* definition of your topic becomes *their* definition. You have the honor of setting the standard for their understanding of your topic.

So answer the Beginners' "What is ___?" questions with care. Help your Beginners with useful, valuable content that answers their questions, and they'll morph into the next kind of reader.

INTERMEDIATE READERS ASK, "HOW DO I DO [___]?"

Intermediate readers are beyond defining your topic — they understand *what* it is and are ready to learn *how* to put it to use in their lives.

But first, they need your help.

Intermediate readers want to know how to implement what they're learning about your topic.

That's why intermediate readers love any information that's served up in the form of how-to guides, step-by-step articles, checklists, tutorials, or video demonstrations.

Those content formats help them implement your topic to meet their challenges — and to begin experiencing positive outcomes.

Answer "How do I do ___?" questions with helpful how-to content that guides Intermediate readers, so they can apply what they're learning and see results in their own lives.

Intermediate readers can make excellent customers for products or services your business offers. They are starting to see results from the things you've taught them, and they are excited to know more and do more.

Advanced readers ask, "How do I get better at [___]?"

The coveted **Advanced** reader! Why are they coveted? Well, you may not have as many Advanced readers as Beginner or Intermediate. But…

Advanced readers are ready for a transaction. They make excellent customers!

Advanced readers understand your topic, and they've started to use it in their lives. But now they need help to make the most of what you offer, teach, or provide a service for.

They've seen the light, and now they want to see tangible benefits from mastering your topic.

These benefits may look like:

- Increased revenues in their business
- Wider reach for their message or offers
- Better personal or professional relationships
- More robust health and overall wellness
- Decreased stress and a greater sense of balance

Advanced content demonstrates that you and your business can be trusted to deliver a quality experience around your topic. Advanced content shows that you know your stuff.

After delivering advanced content, it's a natural transition to ask readers to purchase an advanced solution. Because you have served these Advanced readers well at every step of their journey, they're willing to trust you enough to take out their wallets and do business with you.

HOW MUCH OF EACH TYPE OF CONTENT SHOULD YOU CREATE?

Keep this Beginner/Intermediate/Advanced approach in mind as you build your content strategy.

Before you begin work on a new piece of content, think about the level of awareness your audience member brings to the topic, so you can craft information that serves them well, whatever their level of awareness. And make sure you keep all three groups supplied with content on a regular basis!

To draw a steady stream of prospects to your business, create Beginner content consistently — even when you're tired of writing such basic material. Beginners are actively searching for answers. Let your website become their favorite resource.

You don't need to create quite as much Intermediate and Advanced content. There will be fewer people who fit into these groups.

Here's my loose guesstimate for how much of each type of content you should aim to create. Your mileage may vary — look at your site traffic and results, and then adjust accordingly.

BEGINNER CONTENT: 50%

Tailor about 50% of your content to Beginners. Remember: Beginners want to know the answers to these types of questions:

- What is [YOUR TOPIC]?
- Why is [YOUR TOPIC] important?
- What do I need to understand to use [YOUR TOPIC] in my life?
- How do others use [YOUR TOPIC]?
- What's happening in the world of [YOUR TOPIC] that I need to know about?

INTERMEDIATE CONTENT: 30%

Plan to write about 30% of your content for Intermediate readers. Remember, they're in implementation mode! That means they will gobble up anything you can give them to help put your topic to use in their lives. They are looking for answers to:

- How can I use [YOUR TOPIC] in my day-to-day life?
- What are the best tools to use when I want to work with [YOUR TOPIC]?
- What basic skills do I need to master for [YOUR TOPIC] to give me results?

- What's the step-by-step process I should follow to use [SOME ASPECT OF YOUR TOPIC]?

ADVANCED CONTENT: 20%

Your Advanced readers are well beyond defining your topic and starting to implement it. They are fired up about it and ready to "go pro" with their knowledge. They may plan to use your topic in their business or to make a major upgrade to their lives.

Remember: Advanced readers are thoroughly convinced about the value of mastering your topic. They make excellent customers because they are highly engaged and ready to see better results — *now.* They're wondering:

- What high-level skill do I need to master to profit from [YOUR TOPIC]?
- How can I boost the results I get from [YOUR TOPIC]?
- What do I need to learn if I want to "go pro" and earn revenue with [YOUR TOPIC]?

IS SETTING YOUR CONTENT STRATEGY A ONCE-AND-DONE TASK?

It would be so convenient to sit down and map out a content strategy before you launch a new site while taking your Beginner, Intermediate, and Advanced readers into account. Then — map in hand — you'd simply build out the strategy with every piece of content you create.

The reality, though, tends to be a lot messier than that. *And that's alright.*

I see content marketing as a creative act. Creative acts tend to be messy around the edges. You may start out with a firm plan, but things happen along the way that cause you to pivot and head off in a slightly different direction.

And by *things*, I mean:

- Feedback from the flesh-and-blood readers you attract
- Business opportunities you decide to explore
- New audiences you want to draw to your products and services
- Cultural or business world changes you need to respond to

Try not to feel frustrated by this. Business is all about adaptation and iteration — and your content must adapt and iterate right alongside your business.

Besides, sometimes these direction changes lead to the most interesting, fruitful places! Just check in with yourself and your website analytics on a regular basis to be sure your content is generally pushing you closer to the place you want to go. Don't create content blindly.

This all sounds rather abstract, doesn't it? Time to look at some examples to make this advice easier to apply.

FOR EXAMPLE: A CONTENT PLAN FOR YOUNG SINGLES LEARNING HOW TO COOK

Let's say you are writing content for a website that helps young single people learn how to cook. Let's spell out a simple content plan.

Content for Beginners. You grow awareness and serve Beginners with content that defines cooking techniques, like these:

- Defrosting 101: Safe, Easy, and Quick Ways to Bring Your Frozen Foods to Temperature
- How "Blanching" Will Help You Eat Fresher Foods Next Winter
- What to Cook for Your Date Who Eats Vegan

Make this content freely available, and use it to attract people who are interested in your site's topic. This draws the *right* people to your site — and you can invite those people to join an email list to get more in-depth information and regular updates from your business.

Content for Intermediates. Your Intermediate readers are focused on building their skills so they can implement what they're learning about your topic. In this case, they're looking for ways to make cooking an enjoyable part of their everyday lives:

- How to Sauté Your Way to a 20-Minute Dinner
- Baste Like a Boss: Moister Meats and Vegetables Await
- Golden Goodness: How to Broil Anything in 3 Simple Steps

You could make this information freely available on the web. But it's helpful enough that it could become an opt-in incentive — an ebook or autoresponder course that's delivered to them by email when they join your email list.

Content for the Advanced. You guide Advanced readers toward mastery by providing high-level training — both free and paid — to help them meet their cooking goals:

- Knife Skills for Everyday Cooking [free content]
- 24 Breakfast Recipes You Can Prepare the Night Before [free content, an opt-in incentive, or inexpensive paid content]

- How to Plan, Shop For, and Prepare a Year's Worth of Delicious Meals [paid content]

Depending on how in-depth the content goes, you can choose to make it freely available or offer it for sale. Generally, the more in-depth and comprehensive the solution, the more people are willing to pay for it.

CHECKLIST | SERVE YOUR SITE VISITORS WITH TARGETED CONTENT

Your website visitors arrive on your site with different levels of awareness about your topic. These levels of awareness reflect their readiness to do business with you! As a content creator, you want to be sure to serve everyone, no matter what stage they're in.

- Beginners have lots of basic questions, so create content that answers "What is ___?" and "Why is ___ important?" queries
- Intermediate readers want to begin applying your topic to their lives, so create content that answers their "How do I do ___?" questions
- Advanced readers want high-level information. Create content that answers questions like, "How can I profit from ___?" and "How can I boost the results I get from ___?"
- The exact amount of content you create for each of these groups will vary depending on your current business goals and the audience you are trying to attract.

Keep in mind that Intermediate and Advanced readers make excellent customers, so create content for them in the lead-up to any marketing promotions you may have planned. More on promotions in the next chapter.

11

FIT PROMOTIONS INTO YOUR CONTENT STRATEGY

THE BEST CONTENT STRATEGY MEETS YOUR AUDIENCE'S NEEDS, taking into account their levels of awareness. If you're running a for-profit business or want to have a healthy nonprofit organization, your content strategy should also meet your business promotion needs.

How do you weave those two together? That's what this chapter is about.

If you are involved in marketing your products, services, or events, you likely have some kind of promotions calendar, even if you're only mapping it out a few months at a time. If you know you'll be promoting a specific product or service on predetermined dates, take this into account as you plan your publishing schedule.

Weave together content that attracts the kind of people who will be interested in your upcoming promotion. Capture interested people on an email list with content — and content upgrades — tailored to attract people who will want the upcoming item you plan to offer.

That's content strategy in action!

Here's what that can look like, using the example from the previous chapter: a website devoted to teaching young single people how to cook.

Let's imagine this website is about to offer a new product — a course that teaches inexperienced cooks how to put together easy meals quickly.

SIX WEEKS BEFORE LAUNCHING THE FAB MEALS FAST ONLINE COURSE

Below, we'll invent a content plan for the six-week period before this online course opens its doors.

6 WEEKS TO LAUNCH: PROMOTION-RELATED POST

Headline: 15 in 20: Fifteen Meals You Can Make in 20 Minutes or Less

Content: Feature five of the fifteen recipes online and offer to send the full 15-recipe ebook free when they add their name to the email list of people who'll find out first about the Fab Meals Fast online course.

Purpose: This piece of content is created to attract people through valuable information and move those who are interested in knowing more onto a prospects list you'll use once the course is available for sale.

5 WEEKS TO LAUNCH: REGULAR POST WITH A CALL TO ACTION

Headline: Too Hot to Handle: How to Broil Anything in 3 Simple Steps

Content: Share your best broiling how-to information. At the bottom of the piece, let people know that they can find out first about the Fab Meals Fast online course when they put their name on the email interest list. As a bonus, they'll get the *15 in 20* ebook.

Purpose: This content is similar to the previous piece — you're continuing to offer value and move interested people onto a prospects list.

4 WEEKS TO LAUNCH: PROMOTION-RELATED POST

Headline: How Learning to Cook Can Help You Get Healthy, Find Love, and Enjoy Life

Content: A manifesto-style piece about why you feel strongly that everyone should learn to cook, even if they weren't taught how when they were younger.

With this content, begin to meet common objections. In this case, people may feel they aren't cut out for cooking — that they don't have what it takes.

That objection would stop them from buying the Fab Meals Fast online course. In this piece, weave in stories, case studies, and data that support the idea that *anyone* can learn to cook and everyone should.

Include a strong call to action to join the email list of people who'll find out first about the Fab Meals Fast online course. Promise them they'll get the free *15 in 20* ebook when they sign up.

Purpose: This free content should begin to meet common objections and continue to move interested people onto your interest list.

3 WEEKS TO LAUNCH: REGULAR POST WITH A CALL TO ACTION

Headline: Defrosting 101: Safe, Easy, and Quick Ways to Bring Your Frozen Foods to Temperature

Content: Share your best defrosting how-to tutorial.

Meet another common objection with this content. One almost universal objection is "I don't have time to spare."

In the case of this audience, your piece can demonstrate how delicious foods don't have to take long to prepare, especially if the main ingredients are properly defrosted and ready to cook.

Remind people about the upcoming course, and give them a place to join the interest list. Feature a cover shot of the *15 in 20* ebook they'll get when they sign up.

Purpose: This free content continues to meet common objections and moves interested people onto the email prospects list you'll make a special offer to soon.

2 WEEKS TO LAUNCH: PROMOTION-RELATED POST THAT BUILDS YOUR CASE

Headline: How Reggie Grey Went from Fast Food to Quick, Healthy Meals in Just One Month

Content: This piece is designed to share a case study that will inspire prospective buyers. When you sell online education, the primary objection is often time-related. Your prospects may be thinking *I don't have time to take this course* or *I'll do the first couple of lessons, life will get busy, and I'll never finish.*

In this piece, share uplifting information about how learning this new skill doesn't involve a large time investment and how it could pay off for the rest of their lives.

Use your case study to show how this played out in the life of one of your students.

Include a strong call to action to join the email list of people who'll find out first about the Fab Meals Fast online course, and let them know it's just about to launch.

Purpose: This free content makes a strong case for the product you're about to offer, and it gives people one last chance to join the interest list.

1 WEEK TO LAUNCH: LAUNCH-RELATED POST

Headline: Announcing Fab Meals Fast: Discover Quick and Easy Methods to Master Your Meals and Get Healthy Now

Content: The day before this piece runs, email the people on the interest list for the Fab Meals Fast online course. Offer them an exclusive discount, but only if they sign up in the next 24 hours.

In this piece, you'll announce to the general public that the course is open. To motivate people to make a decision, open the doors to the course for a limited time — say, a week.

Purpose: This content announces your new course and creates a sense of urgency by communicating the deadline for registration.

As you can see, a content plan like the one above weaves together content with a purpose — you're attracting the right prospects for your new offer, inviting them to join an interest list, and then making them an offer once the course is ready.

You're gathering the right audience for the offer you're about to make and gradually moving them from interest to purchase.

At the same time, you're not alienating those audience members who have no desire to buy a cooking course. The information you deliver that's related to your promotion will still be helpful to those who never sign up for the course.

HOW TO USE CONTENT TO HEAD OFF OBJECTIONS AND QUELL FEARS

A smart way to use the lead-up time to a promotion is to think ahead about all the reasons your prospects could decide your offer isn't for them.

To pinpoint the right objections, think about both their external reasons and their internal reasons for not buying.

External reasons to not buy:

- I don't have time to use the product or service
- I don't have money to spend on this offer
- My spouse or business partner won't support this

Internal reasons to not buy:

- I don't have the discipline to make this work
- I'm not 100% clear on my next step, and I don't want to make a move until I'm sure
- I don't think I'm smart/young/fast/hardworking/___ enough

Your job during the pre-launch stage is to publish content that reassures potential buyers about anything that might stop them from giving your offer a chance.

Examples of perfect pre-launch warm-up content:

- **A live video interview** with a customer who shares how they spent a few hours learning your process and saw a difference right away. *Message: You don't have to spend much time to see improvements.*
- **An email newsletter article** that shares a quick and simple

solution that's related to your offer and that people can implement now. *Message: Anyone can do this!*

- **A blog post** that details the money saved when people invest in a solution similar to your offer. *Message: This solution is a worthwhile investment.*
- **A written interview** with a past customer that describes their challenge before buying your product or service and shares how they took a chance, made the purchase, and got great results. *Message: This works for anyone, including people just like you.*

CHECKLIST | FIT PROMOTIONS INTO YOUR CONTENT STRATEGY

The core recommendation in this chapter is to look ahead on your calendar, map out what you plan to promote, and then build content that naturally leads people toward appreciating the solution you're going to offer them, but without alienating audience members who aren't interested in the offer.

- Consider creating an email interest list of people who raise their hands (and furnish their email addresses) to find out more about your upcoming offer
- Create a special price or "first dibs" offer just for your interest list
- To entice people to join the email interest list, create in-depth content on the topic your upcoming offer is about and offer it in exchange for adding their email address to the list
- Create purposeful content in the lead-up to your launch — see the example in this chapter for how to do this over a 6-week pre-launch period
- In the lead-up to your offer, weave together content that meets common objections, offers how-to information,

and generally builds enthusiasm for the solution you'll offer.

There's a lot you can do to engage prospects in the lead-up to a launch. Text, audio, video, and images can all combine to deliver powerful information that establishes your authority and meets their objections before they even surface. There's much more on harnessing the power of multimedia content in the next part, so keep going!

PART III
SUPERCHARGE YOUR CONTENT IMPACT

A FLEXIBLE APPROACH TO CONTENT PLANNING

DEAR PUBLISHER, COME FLY WITH ME, JUST FOR A MOMENT.

Let's imagine that we're cruising high above your website at the 30,000-foot level. From way up here, we can see your big business goals. We look ahead to the horizon and can easily make out the direction we're going.

Now let's descend to the 10,000-foot level. We hover above your website and can make out a few details about your major efforts. We can see your promotion schedule, and we can pick up on any seasons and holidays that may affect the direction of your content.

At these higher altitudes, we don't see the day-to-day process or the tiny decisions you make as you publish your high-impact content.

Now, let's plant our boots on the ground. Your day-to-day content habits affect:

- How you'll get content created — the habits you'll adopt
- How you'll research and add in keyword phrases

- Where you'll interlink your content (linking back to older content and linking forward from older to newer content)
- How you'll spruce up your content visually with images and formatting
- When you'll expand on your content with multimedia additions like video and audio
- How you'll target your content to your audience members' level of awareness

And finally, as mentioned in Chapter 1, your boots-on-the-ground day-to-day habits will be impacted by the lifecycle of your site. Your content goals will change as you move from the early days through the middle years and into the mature stage of your website.

YOUR DAY WON'T LOOK LIKE ANY OTHER CONTENT CREATOR'S DAY

With all these variables to keep in mind, it's important to remember that there's no single approach to content creation that will work for everyone.

You don't have to have your editorial calendar completely decided at the beginning of the year. There's a certain amount of flexibility that needs to happen in any editorial plan. And you want to be sure you adapt your content plans to the feedback you're getting from your audience.

> *Use the "30,000-foot, 10,000-foot, and boots-on-the-ground" approach when you look at your editorial calendar, too.*

Map out your general direction at the beginning of the year. Then nail down actual topics when you are looking at each quarter on your editorial calendar. Write headlines and begin researching content once you are looking at a single month. More on this in Chapter 16.

As you move through this part, think of it as a menu of options for you to explore. Remember where you are in your website lifecycle, what promotions you have coming up, and what kind of people you want to attract.

Pick up free bonus materials that will help you develop your "30,000-foot, 10,000-foot, and boots-on-the-ground" approach at MasterContentStrategy.com/bonus

REPURPOSING CONTENT FOR FUN, PROFIT & TRAFFIC

IN THIS CHAPTER, I'M GOING TO INTRODUCE HOW YOU CAN maximize the impact and reach of every piece of content you create with a variety of content repurposing ideas. It's easy when you have repurposing in mind from the very beginning of your content creation process.

My not-so-secret goal is to get you thinking about repurposing from the start. To think ahead so you can multiply the impact of the content you create.

Here's what we'll cover in this chapter:

- **The benefits of repurposing content.** Repurposed content gets more reach because it appears on more platforms. Multimedia content takes extra time to consume — and search engines love to see people spending more time on your page, and they may reward you with higher standing in their results.
- **A simple content repurposing strategy.** It starts while you're mapping out your content backbone — we'll make

repurposing a natural part of your content creation process.

- **Content repurposing examples.** I'll give you lots of options to choose from, so you can pick one or two to explore.

JUST STARTING TO CREATE CONTENT? FILE THESE IDEAS AWAY FOR NOW

First, let's state the obvious: If you're having trouble getting content created or you are in the very early days of content creation, please read this chapter now, but plan to use these concepts in the future. The concept of "maximizing your content impact" may feel a little overwhelming if you're still struggling to get your basic content created.

If you are in the early days of your website, and if you haven't already, read the Content Marketing Crash Course part of this book. If you need more guidance, grab your very own copy of my book, *Master Content Marketing*. It was written to help content marketing beginners, and it will help you structure and create content that attracts an audience and grows your business. The structure you'll learn will make repurposing content much faster!

Once you're comfortable with the basic content creation process, it's time to maximize the impact your content has on the world.

The internet is a noisy place, and these content repurposing tips will help get your content in front of more people — in more places — so you can drive traffic back to your online business.

DOES REPURPOSING REFER TO REPUBLISHING CONTENT ON OTHER PLATFORMS?

Some people think "repurposing" means taking content you already created and republishing it as is on another platform. I call that *syndicating* your content, not *repurposing* your content.

For example, syndicated television shows appear on one network when they're first broadcast, and then they are rerun on other platforms — other network channels, Netflix, Hulu — in their original form.

It's not a bad idea to take, say, a blog post and copy/paste it into LinkedIn, Medium, or Quora to reach a different audience with your already-created content.

But that's not what we're covering in this chapter. In this chapter, we're talking about taking the content you created and *transforming* it into a new format. You can embed that new format within your original content, and host it in other places, as well.

This is about *transforming* your content as you repurpose it — turning it into a different type of media or extracting an excerpt to share elsewhere.

WHY SHOULD I BOTHER REPURPOSING CONTENT?

Because it's good for you and good for your audience.

Repurposing content is a good use of your content production time. Here's why…

> *Rather than create yet another brand-new piece of content and add it to the mountain of information that's already available online, I'm asking you to create only exceptional content — and give it much greater impact by repurposing it.*

Repurposing, in this case, means rethinking your content so it will reach people in a variety of places using a wide range of content formats. That means…

Written content becomes:

- Image-based content
- Audio content
- Video content

Audio content becomes:

- Image-based content
- Written content
- Video content

Video content becomes:

- Image-based content
- Written content
- Audio content

After all, we're not all readers or all podcast listeners or all video watchers. We are each of these things at different moments. When you serve up your content in lots of different formats, you reach people no matter where they are or how much time they have available to absorb your information.

For example, someone may have time to read your long article in the morning, but prefer to watch your video during an afternoon break. Depending on the time of day, they may quickly flip through your slide deck or leisurely peruse Pinterest and click your pinned image to read more. They could skim your blog post's subheads and images, then bookmark it to read later. Or they may take time to listen to your topic in audio form during their workout or commute.

A person's format preference might depend on how they learn best — or it might simply be a function of the time of day.

Content repurposing means you give every piece of content you create the maximum impact it can have by using it in many different ways. Making this extra effort should drive more people to your website and expand your reach.

HOW LONG DOES IT TAKE TO REPURPOSE CONTENT?

If you map out your content repurposing plans while you're in the content planning stages, it won't be too time-consuming.

Remember how we talked about your Day 1 tasks in the "lazy" 4-Day Content Creation System? They were:

- Create an irresistible headline that will get clicked
- Write your subheads and think through your content structure

As you create this basic structure — the backbone — for your piece of content, think about how your content would benefit from a video, audio, or additional visual content, like a slide deck or an image gallery.

When looking at your content structure, here are some ideas for where you can repurpose your information to enrich the content experience:

- If one section of your content mentions a complex task, consider creating a quick tutorial to show how it's done
- If you mention a few thought leaders in your content,

consider recording a quick audio interview and embedding that in your content

- If your content is audio or video, create a checklist or resource list and include its link on the page
- If you'd like to summarize your information, do it in a slide deck that you embed at the end of your article

There are many more ideas like these ahead in this chapter, so keep reading.

When you develop a tried-and-true method, repurposing your content shouldn't add more than an hour or so to your total content creation time.

And your posts will be richer, more valuable, and more engaging. It's well worth it if it means you'll spend less time creating new content and more time maximizing the impact of content you've already created.

WHAT'S THE MINIMUM AMOUNT OF CONTENT REPURPOSING I SHOULD DO?

If you are tight on time, plan to focus on repurposing your content on the one off-site platform where you've already gathered an audience. If the content takes off, you can expand to other media types and platforms.

For example, if you've gathered a following on YouTube, focus on including embedded YouTube videos in your written content. Or if you have lots of followers on LinkedIn, explore repurposing your content on SlideShare, which is owned by the company.

Let's say you have quite a following on Facebook. Consider delivering a Facebook Live video with your content providing the topic and talking points. Or try writing a meaty Facebook post where you summarize one section of your content and share a link back to the full piece.

> *The bare minimum content repurposing you should do is to focus on giving your content maximum play on your most successful off-site platform.*

But of course, I'd love to see you do even more than that. Read on to learn how…

Your vow of simplicity

As you add content repurposing to your content creation routine, here's what I want you to keep in mind:

Master one content repurposing habit at a time. Use one method for a while and track your results. If repurposing your content on the platform you've chosen is sending significant traffic to your site, consider adding another media type if you have the mental bandwidth.

Think outside the format box. Content repurposing has the biggest impact when you engage different senses with the new formats. More on this ahead in the Idea Bank.

HOW CAN I STRUCTURE MY CONTENT SO IT'S EASY TO REPURPOSE?

Well-structured content — like the kind outlined in the 4-Day Content Creation System — lends itself to repurposing because it's divided up logically and builds its points in a smooth flow from beginning to end.

Having an underlying content structure is the key to making this whole thing easy. For example, you can extract one section of an article, complete with its subheads, and make it:

- The topic of a social media post, as outlined previously
- Something you riff about in a live video
- A topic you dig into in a podcast interview

Well-structured, logical content is super easy to repurpose! More on this in the ideas that follow.

EXAMPLES OF REPURPOSED CONTENT YOU CAN CREATE FROM WELL-STRUCTURED ORIGINAL CONTENT

If you're not sure which media type to use to start, use the rule of thumb already mentioned — start with the platform you have the most traction on.

Here's something else to consider: Build on your media creation strengths. If recording audio is easy-peasy but creating an image makes you break out in a sweat, stick with audio. If building a slide deck is no big deal, but you can't stand the sound of your own voice, don't record audio — build that slide deck!

You get the picture. At first, aim for a frictionless content repurposing experience by creating content for your most-visited platform with the content type you're most comfortable creating. You can always explore new platforms and content formats later.

A few examples of how to translate your content structure into repurposed content:

- **Slide decks** using the headline as a cover slide, the subheads as divider slides, with your main content in between
- **Video content** using the headline as a splash screen, the

subheads as video segments, and the main content as your talking points
- **Podcast content** using the headline as your theme, the subheads as main topics to cover, and the main content as the details you'll talk about

From these examples, you can see that if you start with well-structured content, it will make your repurposing task easy and fast.

CONTENT REPURPOSING IDEA BANK: THREE APPROACHES TO TRY

The ideas here are meant to get you thinking about how to morph your content from one type of media to another. Find your go-to media type in the list below and get inspired by the ideas shared here.

Remember: Find repurposing methods that build on your current strengths and comfort level.

REPURPOSE YOUR WRITTEN CONTENT

Here's an astonishing fact:

People following directions with text and illustrations do 323% better than people following text-only directions, according to a study in Educational Technology Research and Development.

Written content packs more information per second of consumption than anything else. You can't beat text for efficient delivery!

But when you pair written content with other media types, engagement and time-on-page soar.

Making your written content visual can help illuminate your meaning and add an emotional impact to your words. When you take your written words and condense the main points into easy-to-grasp signature branded images — images with text, your brand colors, and your business name — you'll boost the impact of your information and your brand.

For more on signature branded images and how to use them to market your business, search on the BIG Brand System site. It's a topic I've covered many times.

IDEAS FOR REPURPOSING WRITTEN CONTENT

Remember: That underlying structure you gave to your content — the headline and subheads you wrote — gives you an easy starting point to take your words and turn them into something else. Try these ideas to transform your written content into:

Image-based content:

- **Create a slide deck with the article's main points.** Use your subheads as a guide. Share the slide deck on LinkedIn, SlideShare, and other social platforms where you've developed a following.
- **Make signature branded images.** Extract important quotes or information from the article, overlay them on images, and use the assembled images to promote the content on social media platforms.
- **Reuse these images in your email marketing** to drive readers to your article.
- **Create visuals to illustrate data.** Charts and graphs give your numbers a visual form that's easy to grasp in a single glance. Embed these on the page and share them on social

platforms to engage people and make them want to click through to get the whole story.

- **Use images to illustrate important points in the article.** Use images to divide major sections in longer pieces of content, and then use these images to share the content on social media platforms.

Audio content:

- **Record your written content.** Sit down in front of a microphone, introduce yourself and your website, and read your article — with great enthusiasm and inflection, please! Make this audio file downloadable so listeners can consume your content on the go. If you'd rather not record your own voice, explore automated solutions like Amazon Polly, which reads your page content to site visitors.

Video content:

- **Drop key points into an online video creator** designed for non-video folks. Platforms change year by year, but some tried-and-true providers are Animoto, Adobe Spark, and Lumen5.
- **Turn on your camera and talk!** You are likely sitting just a few feet from a camera. If you're comfortable with it, consider doing a live video where you share the most important points in your article. If you'd rather practice and polish your presentation, record it in advance and post it.
- **Use these content-based videos** on social media platforms to drive attention and traffic back to your article. They can be embedded back inside the article to give your readers a chance to feel more connected to you.

- **Use screenshots from your videos** to promote your written content in your email marketing.
- **Create and present a webinar based on your article.** This is something I do all the time with my blog content and free Brown Bag Workshops. I use the blog post to organize my thoughts around a topic, and then I present the same topic in webinar form using the article's underlying structure to create the presentation outline and slides.

"Best of" content:

- **Quote yourself.** Extract the most-compelling sentences from your article, drop them between quote marks, and share this content on social media.
- **Create an autoresponder course** based on your written content and drip out your information one short email at a time.
- **Write long-form social media posts** which deliver one section of your information at a time, published over several days.

If people don't have time to absorb your epic written content all at once, help them benefit from your information by repurposing the main points into digestible chunks that are delivered as images, audio, video, and excerpts.

When you give your words life in different forms, you'll increase the number of entry points people can use to find and enjoy your amazing written content.

REPURPOSE YOUR AUDIO CONTENT

Podcasts are hot right now, but they're notoriously single-platform. One challenge? They're often consumed on the go and while doing other activities like exercise, housework, or driving. This makes adding multimedia elements challenging. You don't want your call to action to cause people to drive off the road!

It's not easy to ask listeners to make the leap from their audio player to your website. But when you stack valuable content on the episode pages you host on your site, they'll find themselves stopping what they're doing to search out your additional resources.

IDEAS FOR REPURPOSING AUDIO CONTENT

Read on to discover ways to add complementary content to your audio — and to make the repurposed content easy to find with just a click.

Image-based content:

- **Make signature branded images.** Extract important quotes or information from the audio, overlay them on images, and use the assembled images to promote your audio content on social media platforms.
- **Reuse these images in your email marketing** to drive readers to your audio.
- **Illustrate data quoted in the audio** and include the charts and graphs on the episode page.

Written content:

- **Have your audio transcribed** so it becomes readable. Services like Rev.com (transcription by a person) and

Temi.com (cheaper, less accurate transcription by machine) make this easy. Post the transcript on your episode page so search engines can index the keywords in your audio content and drive traffic to your page. *Note: Proofread all transcripts before posting them! Make sure you review them to confirm that proper names are spelled correctly and all the information is clear.*

- **Create a slide deck** with the audio's key takeaways using your underlying structure to create the structure for your slides. Share this on LinkedIn, SlideShare, and other social platforms where you've developed a following.
- **Create content upgrades** for your audio content. Help listeners implement what they're learning when you create a checklist, worksheet, or resource guide that complements the audio topic. *Bonus: Ask for an email address in exchange for this complementary information and grow your email list while you increase engagement.*

Video content:

- **Create video from your audio.** Use your podcast art as the splash screen for your video content. Create simple slides with the most important points and record yourself clicking through them to make a video. Post this on YouTube, social media platforms, and embed it on the episode page on your site.
- **Drop important quotes into a video creator** designed for non-video folks. Platforms change year by year, but some tried-and-true providers are Animoto, Adobe Spark, and Lumen5.
- **Create your audio on camera!** Some podcast hosts, like Joanna Penn of TheCreativePenn.com, conduct their podcast interviews on camera. This allows her to extract the audio to use as a podcast and also create a transcript

that's published as written content on her site. Joanna's a content repurposing pro!

Most importantly, if you're a podcast creator, establish an easy-to-remember naming convention for your podcast episode pages. You want to be able to say simply, "Go to mysite.com forward slash seven to find all the extra content for episode seven."

REPURPOSE YOUR VIDEO CONTENT

Any time you add motion to your information, you can expect your audience to spend more time with your content and become more engaged with what you're sharing. And yet, people have a love-hate relationship with video.

On the one hand, it's dynamic and helps them feel a genuine sense of connection to the brave soul who positioned themselves in front of the lens.

On the other hand, unless you're a professional on-air talent, your viewers may get frustrated when they see your presentation wander off target, or you take too long to get to the point.

What can you offer your less-than-enthusiastic video viewers to help them get the most out of your information? Structure!

Consider adding visual dividers to your video content. These can be a screen overlay or a moving graphic which introduces the next segment of content — the equivalent of a subhead in an article. This adds words to your video, and it will help viewers process the information you're presenting. Remember, if you've created a content backbone through a headline and subheads, your dividers will already be mapped out.

Ideas for repurposing video content

You can also offer a variety of formats for the readers and listeners in your audience:

Written content:

- **Create a transcript for your video** using Rev.com, Temi.com, or software like Descript. Post this on your own website along with an embedded video so that search engines can index the keywords in your video content.
- **Create a blog post from your transcript.** Take a clean transcript and format it with subheads, bulleted lists, and blockquotes, and add an image.
- **Add captions to your video** using the built-in captioning capabilities on platforms like YouTube and Facebook (you'll have to clean them up). Converting video to readable text helps people follow along if they're unable to hear its audio. You can also use software like Descript, or simply hire someone to listen and transcribe what you're saying.

Audio content:

- **Create a podcast from your video.** Aim for crystal clear audio that you can extract and upload as a podcast episode. For inspiration, see the note about Joanna Penn's brilliant working process in the previous section.

Image-based content:

- **Use screenshots from your videos** to create still images you can use to promote the video content in your email marketing and on social media. *If humor is a part of your* *brand story, bonus points if you screen capture an awkward moment.*

- **Make signature branded images.** Extract important quotes or information from the video, overlay them on images, and use the assembled images to promote the content on social media platforms.
- **Reuse these images in your email marketing** to drive viewers to your video.

"Best of" content:

- **Edit videos into short highlight clips** and repurpose these on social media platforms to entice viewers to watch the full video.
- **Replay video excerpts during a webinar presentation.** Many webinar software platforms allow you to play pre-recorded videos. This is ideal if you need to demonstrate software, offer a tutorial, or give a site tour. Recording these ahead of time will ensure the final product is engaging and glitch-free.

REMEMBER, YOU DON'T NEED TO DO ALL OF THESE! THIS IS AN idea bank, so pick one or two ways to explore repurposing your primary content for other platforms that will help you expand your reach.

All of the above happens before or around the time of content publication. Our final approach is all about how to repurpose your content for the long haul…

CHECKLIST | REPURPOSING CONTENT FOR FUN, PROFIT & TRAFFIC

Repurposing content means giving your information new life (and additional attention) by transforming it into a different format from its original. As you become a more confident content creator, mastering content repurposing is a natural next step in your development.

- Repurposing is easier when your content uses an underlying structure like the one taught in the Content Marketing Crash Course part of this book, and it's covered in detail in *Master Content Marketing*
- Aim to explore one or two content repurposing techniques at a time
- Start with your most-used content format and use the ideas here to select a way you'll change it into a fresh, new format
- Base your new format selection — and its platform — on what you believe will appeal to the ideal customer you want to reach
- Make content visual, make it move, make it digestible, make it easy to find, and keep promoting it over time

Please don't let these ideas overwhelm you if you're just starting out. Content repurposing isn't for new content creators — it's a technique you can use on a growing and mature site as you master content marketing.

BUILD A CONTENT AMPLIFICATION STRATEGY

MARK SCHAEFER IS ONE OF THE HEAVY-HITTING THOUGHT leaders in the content marketing industry. He's a multi-time author, an in-demand speaker, and a college professor.

Back in 2014, Mark wrote a piece of content called "Content Shock: Why content marketing is not a sustainable strategy."

It shook up every content marketer on the internet. Some were more worried than others — but just about everyone noticed.

Mark's renowned post popularized the concept of *content shock.* He proposed that we had arrived at a time when simply creating well-crafted content was not enough. He said that if you follow the basic laws of supply and demand, the ability to *consume* content is finite — there are only so many hours in a day. And the ability to *create* content (and the amount of content being created) is increasing at a faster rate than our attention spans.

> *Too much content supply with not enough content demand is a recipe for content shock.*

By 2015, Mark had data to back up this claim. His blog post "Content Shock is here. Now what?" noted that major sites publishing top-quality content were seeing drops in social shares, comments, and traffic.

Mark recommended that we be more strategic about content *promotion, distribution,* and *advertising* to give our information the best chance of being found.

By 2017, Mark had even more evidence of content shock. But in "Content shock re-visited, the content marketing myths and realities," he was also beginning to feel optimistic. He said, "the economic value of content that is not seen and shared is zero." But he also said the tools for promoting and distributing content had multiplied.

He called content marketing "a war for attention," and said we should spend as much time thinking about how we'll *amplify* our content as we do creating it.

Content amplification is what we'll focus on in this chapter. When you publish new content, people won't automatically appear to read, listen, or watch. It's not enough to simply publish.

If you want your content to be found and used, you must advocate for it like you're its biggest fan. That's right: The first and most important person who must advocate for the content you've worked so hard to create is *you*. So give it a good chance with the ideas you'll find here.

HOW TO CREATE AN AMPLIFICATION STRATEGY FOR EVERY PIECE YOU PUBLISH

Simply publishing a strong piece of content is not enough to get it seen. Some research says that more than 2 million blog posts are published *every day*.

I don't say this to discourage you, I promise. I say it so you'll go into your amplification planning with your eyes wide open to the reality out there.

> *Competition is fierce, and you must advocate for your content if you want it to be found.*

In the previous chapter, we dug deep into content repurposing, and I shared dozens of ideas for transforming your content to give it a wider reach. Now, we'll cover amplification techniques you can use for every piece of content you publish. We'll talk about:

- Cultivating a presence on social media
- Emailing new content to your subscribers
- Sharing your high-quality content with thought leaders
- Paying to promote your best content
- Repurposing content as an amplification strategy

I'm now seeing more content marketing thought leaders advocate for spending as much time amplifying your content as you do creating it. I'm not sure if this is based on hard data, but the idea is valid — content amplification matters, so make it a part of your content creation routine from the very beginning.

THE ROLE OF DOMAIN AUTHORITY

By the end of 2017, Mark started talking about *domain authority* in relation to content marketing. Domain authority is basically a grade that search engines give your website. No one knows the exact criteria, but as Mark says, it's thought to be a combination of...

- **The age of your website:** How many years has it been online?

- **The size of your website:** How many pages of content does it contain?
- **Backlink quality:** Are high-quality websites linking to your website?
- **Outbound link quality:** Is your website's page content linking out to respected websites?
- **Content relevance:** Is your content consistently on topic?
- **Keyword use:** Do your keyword phrases match searches — and are those phrases used throughout your content?
- **Publishing consistency:** Is your website updated with fresh content on a regular basis?

Here's the thing: A solid content marketing strategy helps with all of the items in the list above. You'll add consistent, relevant content on a regular basis. This should boost your domain authority for as long as you keep it up, giving you better results month after month.

HOW TO USE SOCIAL MEDIA

DEVELOP AND USE AT LEAST ONE SOCIAL NETWORK

Just like the concept of content shock has made us realize that time to consume content isn't growing at the same pace that content creation is moving, we've realized that if people want to live their lives and accomplish anything, they can't spend all day on social networks.

But in the early 2000s, it seemed every year brought the birth of a new social network. Those of us building online businesses felt an obligation to be everywhere all at once. It wasn't unusual to see websites try to cultivate audiences on seven or eight different social media platforms.

Thankfully, time and cooler heads have helped us become more thoughtful about our social network use. My advice today?

In the early days of your site, choose one social network to focus on building. Establish a lively audience there before you work on building a presence on another network. What do I mean by "lively?" An audience that responds to the content you post and engages in conversation with you!

Choose the social network you'll develop based on the ideal audience member you want to attract and the content format you're most comfortable with.

Find out which networks are most used by people like your ideal customer. And think hard about whether you're comfortable creating content in the style most used on that network. For example, if appearing on camera makes you terribly uncomfortable, don't amplify your content on YouTube!

As you build your audience on your social network, make content amplification a priority. With each new piece you publish, be sure to share, comment, and repurpose your content on your social network of choice so your audience there sees it as it's released.

I recommend you aim to make a BIG splash on the day you publish, and you continue to beat the ground on days two and three after publication, inviting people to click through and read, listen, or watch. That means heavy repetition on social media platforms — if you're afraid you're going to annoy people, you're probably doing it right.

Do social shares and traffic really matter?

This is going to sound like a contrarian view, but I'm going to drop it here in case it's helpful to you. In the end, we're creating content to attract the exact right people to our online homes. We're using that content to move them along a path and prepare them to become loyal, happy customers.

How many Facebook shares your piece gets is not *really* a part of this process.

How many podcast downloads your latest episode gets isn't a part of it, either. These are what we call *vanity metrics*.

> *In the end, what really matters is that your content works to create happy customers for your business. And that your business goals — whether they're revenue or reach — are met with your content.*

The number of social shares a piece gets is a useful metric that may tell you which content is popular. But popular content doesn't necessarily lead to sales.

It's the same thing for traffic, believe it or not. Sometimes we write a piece of content that stumbles its way into a first-page ranking for a specific term in Google, for example. If that piece of content isn't aligned with a step in your customer education and engagement process, your site ends up getting a lot of traffic that doesn't actually help your business.

Social shares and traffic do matter — but last I checked, my bank wouldn't allow me to deposit them in my checking account!

What ultimately matters is to create content that moves people through the levels of awareness — from Beginner to Intermediate to Advanced. You'll know it's working when you see a steady flow of these people moving from visiting your pages to becoming customers.

 Remember: It's those Intermediate and Advanced members of your audience who are primed to become your customers, so focus on developing those groups to grow your business.

AMPLIFY IN THE INBOX WHEN YOU EMAIL YOUR SUBSCRIBERS

As you publish new content, be sure to send it out to your email subscribers.

Back in the day, we used to send an entire piece of content within the email message. Instead, I recommend you send a link to the full post so your audience can absorb it — in all its glory — in its native website environment.

Use your email message to tease the content. Sell it with a scintillating subject line, a peppy intro, and tantalizing bullet points. Write a short preview of your content that highlights what people will learn, why you felt this topic was important to share right now, and how they'll be able to use what they are about to read, listen to, or watch.

Make them want to click through and consume the whole thing!

SHARE YOUR VERY BEST CONTENT WITH THOUGHT LEADERS IN YOUR INDUSTRY

Save this technique for your very best, most comprehensive, evergreen content.

When you've written something you're extra proud of, let your industry's thought leaders know so they can share it. Send a quick message, either to an email address, if you have it, or through a contact form. Let the thought leader know when it was published, and share how their audience will benefit from your content.

Be sure to mention *why* you think their audience might benefit — and do your homework. Mention a recent article they published, a podcast episode you listened to, or a conference where they spoke. This will make your pitch stand out as thoughtful and useful.

PAY TO PROMOTE YOUR BEST CONTENT

Social networks don't provide up-to-date platforms and unlimited bandwidth for new content out of the goodness of their hearts. They're businesses, which means they all have a way you can pay to get your content in front of more people.

It makes sense to do this, especially when you have content that's part of a larger promotional effort which will lead to revenue for your business. This is a move that will bring more people to your business so you can engage with them and move them through your Beginner, Intermediate, and Advanced stages.

The advice here is similar to what we've already talked about: Experiment with paying to promote content on a single platform first. Start with the social network where you've already built an audience, of course.

Each social network's advertising rules are different, but you will get the most impact from your investment if you have an established audience on the platform where you run ads, so master one before you move on to the next.

CONTENT REPURPOSING HELPS YOU MAKE MORE IMPACT

Keep in mind that content repurposing, which we covered in the previous chapter, is an amplification strategy, too. When you morph content from one media type to another, the new media type is often hosted off-site on a different platform. That makes it easy to share your content in — and from — multiple places.

One example of this is a live social media video you create based on a recently published piece of content. That video originates on its social network, but then you can download it from there and upload it to your YouTube channel, you can embed the video on the original piece of content, and you can share a link to it in an email. You can even spread it to other social platforms.

The possibilities are endless, but I urge you to start with your strengths and build on them. Find the media type you feel most comfortable creating and double down on getting really good at it so you can make the most of this amplification strategy.

CHECKLIST | BUILD A CONTENT AMPLIFICATION STRATEGY

In a world of content shock, our content amplification efforts are every bit as important as our content creation efforts. Be strategic about how you'll promote the content you work so hard to build.

- Build domain authority with smart, consistent content creation
- Don't live by vanity metrics like social shares — instead, pay attention to the business results delivered by your content
- Share your content on social media, via email, and — for extra special content — with industry thought leaders
- Consider paying to promote your strategically important content
- Use content repurposing as an amplification strategy

It's challenging to think of yourself as a creator *and* an amplifier. I like to think of it as wearing many hats.

This is one big reason the 4-Day Content Creation System, as taught in Chapter 9, works well. You don't have to create and promote on the same day, which gives you a chance to switch hats — and mindsets — as you move from content creation to content amplification.

15

CONTENT UPGRADES AS EMAIL LIST BUILDERS

THERE'S A RULE OF THUMB THAT HAS MADE THE ROUNDS OF online business owners for many years. Have you heard it? It goes like this:

For every subscriber on your email list, you'll earn $1 per month in your online business.

That plays out like this:

- 750 people on your email list = an income of $750 per month
- 7,500 people on your email list = an income of $7,500 per month
- 75,000 people on your email list = an income of $75,000 per month

Now, I can tell you that I have met many, many online business owners who are exceptions to this rule! They are making excellent income from their small, super-targeted, and highly engaged lists. And there are others who have cultivated a large list of prospects who don't respond to their offers! List size never tells the whole story.

But those numbers make you think, don't they? There is a direct correlation between the number of people you're able to make offers to and the amount of income you can expect your online business to generate.

So, let's build your email list, shall we?

WHY EMAIL ADDRESSES ARE MORE VALUABLE THAN SOCIAL MEDIA FOLLOWERS

Let's clear the air on this topic before we start. You may have seen people talking about all the money they have made from:

- Their Instagram followers
- Their Facebook groups
- Their Pinterest following
- Their YouTube subscribers

I suppose I should resist the urge to be cynical, but we know each other by now, so I think you'll forgive me when I observe that many, many of those folks *also* happen to have a course to sell you where they'll teach you how to *make money on those platforms just like they did!*

And when you dig deep into those courses, guess what most of them recommend?

That you *gather as many people as possible on an email list* so you can engage with your audience in their inboxes.

Here's the thing: Your email marketing list is a business asset you own 100%. Social media networks *lend you space* on their platforms, but they reserve the right to close your account there at any time. That's why I don't recommend that you make a social media network your primary mode of contact with your audience.

I recommend that you build your email list using your content. There are other, more roundabout ways to grow a list, but this is a book about content strategy, and this next technique is a powerful way to use content to grow a targeted, engaged audience you can stay in contact with by email.

UPGRADE ME WITH TARGETED CONTENT

One of the reasons content works so well is that anyone who clicks through to read it — or listen to it or watch it — can be directed to take the next step with a call to action.

They "vote" for your content topic by clicking through to consume it. They vote again if they click on your call to action. And the way to record their votes is to create a content upgrade they can give their ultimate vote to — an email address they share in order to grab what you create.

When you're creating content that leads to a product or service you plan to offer, develop content upgrades so you can build highly targeted lists of email addresses from people who would be interested in your offering.

Use your email marketing program to create an opt-in form that you embed in your piece of content. Then move these subscribers to a specific list, or tag them with a specific term, so you can remember what they voted an interest in.

Let's see what that looks like using a real example.

FOR EXAMPLE: SELLING BIRDHOUSE BLUEPRINTS

If you sell birdhouses and plan to sell a product that features five do-it-yourself birdhouse-building blueprints designed to attract specific types of birds, you can create a content upgrade that will be of great interest to the ideal customer for this offer.

Start by thinking about your ideal customer for this product. What do you know about them?

- They love watching birds
- They enjoy building things
- They likely have time for hobbies

For a content upgrade, you could offer a free ebook titled *How to Build a Visitors Center for Birds Using Items from Your Recycling Bin.*

You write a piece of content about bird migration patterns. You embed an email opt-in form in your content that offers this content upgrade. And you gather a list of people who you know — for sure — are interested in birds and enjoy building things as a hobby.

When your birdhouse blueprints product is ready, the first people you offer it to are the group who signed up for this content upgrade.

SIX CONTENT UPGRADE IDEAS

Content upgrades don't have to be difficult to create to be considered valuable to your audience. People who are interested in a topic are grateful when you boil down information to the essentials for them so they can get results fast. Consider these ideas as you plan your content upgrades:

- 5- to 10-minute video tutorials

- 20-minute audio recordings or interviews with thought leaders
- 1-page checklists for getting things done the right way
- 2-page worksheets that help users make a decision or a plan
- 3-page resource guides featuring the best solutions in your industry
- A single template or swipe file with examples your audience can follow

Email subscribers matter. But targeted, engaged email subscribers? *They're gold!* Use content upgrades to thoughtfully build your list with these high-value subscribers.

CHECKLIST | CONTENT UPGRADES AS EMAIL LIST BUILDERS

Content upgrades are a reliable way to identify people in your audience who are especially interested in a topic you plan to make an offer around. The upgrade expands on the content you're creating with more in-depth information that you offer in exchange for their email address.

- Before creating the upgrade, spend some time thinking about the qualities you're looking for in the ideal customer you want to attract to your offer
- Create a content upgrade that will naturally attract this kind of person
- Less is more! Make a content upgrade that delivers quick results and is easy for you to create
- Embed the opt-in form in your content and use your email marketing program to move these subscribers to a specific list, or tag them with a specific term, so you can remember what they voted an interest in

Grow your list, grow your impact, and grow your revenues with strategic content upgrades. They create a direct line between the content you're creating and the audience you're building.

16

PLAN YEARLY, QUARTERLY, AND MONTHLY CONTENT

Chances are really good that any content plan you map out a year in advance will go through several changes as the year rolls on — *and that's perfectly fine!* The most successful businesses take an agile approach to their content marketing. They respond to changes in the culture and business environment, and to the needs of their prospects and customers. Their content *adapts*.

Here's how to think about it:

- **Your Yearly Content Plan** is a broad overview of what you want your content to accomplish for your business in the coming year
- **Your Quarterly Content Plan** builds the framework with the specific topics you'll cover and when you'll cover them, and
- **Your Monthly Content Plan** is a week-by-week editorial plan you'll use to guide your content creation

In this section, we'll cover how to approach your yearly, quarterly, and monthly content plans.

The good news is the thinking and planning you do for one plan will feed directly into the next. Your Yearly Content Plan builds the vision, your Quarterly Content Plan builds the framework, and your Monthly Content Plan maps out the content you'll create.

The ultimate goal? To completely eliminate what I call "the blank page blues" — that sinking feeling that happens when you realize you need to create a piece of content, and you have no idea what topic you should cover. Say goodbye to that feeling, because these plans will eradicate it completely.

YEARLY CONTENT PLAN: STATE YOUR BIG VISION

Your Yearly Content Plan will look more like a mission statement than a step-by-step plan for reaching your business goals with your content — *and that's fine.* That broad vision will inform the more specific plans that happen next.

To create a Yearly Content Plan, think about your business, and ask yourself these questions:

- What are my most important business goals in the year ahead?
- What offers do I want to promote? (At this point, don't worry about when the promotions will happen.)
- Do I need to attract a different kind of prospect to meet my goals?

If you answered "Yes" to the third question, ask yourself:

- How is this new prospect different from the people who visit my website now?
- What are the challenges this new type of prospect is experiencing? What drives them to search for a site like mine?
- How will my content help them meet their challenges?

The idea here is to come up with a broad description of what your content will attempt to do in the year ahead, and an idea of who you'll target. We'll get more specific in the next stages. For now, set a big goal that you'll aim for.

And remember, this big goal is going to take your website lifecycle into account. For more on that topic, review Chapter 1.

This kind of overview is fun to do toward the end of the calendar year, so you can look back at your entire year of content and take your results into consideration as you plan the year ahead.

QUARTERLY CONTENT PLAN: ADD DATES FOR PROMOTIONS AND EVENTS

Your Quarterly Content Plan will include dates for events like upcoming promotions — business events that will help you meet your goals. You also want to include holidays and cultural happenings that impact how your audience will receive and respond to the offers you make or the content you share.

Don't make the mistake of ignoring the calendar when planning to promote a product or service!

To begin working on your Quarterly Content Plan, ask yourself these questions as you begin attaching content to dates:

- What upcoming major holidays or cultural events will impact my audience?
- What seasonal realities will affect their availability or constrain their time? (Think: summer vacation, produce seasons for cooks, winter holidays, etc.)
- What new products or services do I plan to introduce during this quarter?
- What existing products or services will I promote this quarter?
- When will I introduce these offers?
- What dates encompass the entire promotion period? (Block these out on your calendar.)
- How much warm-up time do I need to allow before I can make this offer?

That last point can be tricky. There's no set answer for how much warm-up time to allow before an offer, but I can share the variables you should keep in mind:

Count all the ways you communicate with your core audience. As you make your Quarterly Content Plan, consider all the communication vehicles you have available. These include your blog content, your email marketing, your social media posts, your podcast, your video series, your live events, and anyplace else you interact with your audience.

Plan to spread the message across all your platforms. Your business is a helpful resource that reaches people in many places. A solid content plan enlists all your platforms in a coordinated effort to inform and remind prospects of your upcoming offer. Share your message across every platform where you've gathered an audience.

Don't be afraid to repeat your message. People are busy, and they see a lot of content besides yours every day. Spread your message out over at least a few weeks and up to a few months. And don't be afraid to repeat your reminders about your upcoming product or service launch — believe me, your audience isn't paying nearly as much attention to it as you are!

It's smart to map out your Quarterly Content Plan at the beginning of the third month in every quarter — a month before the new quarter begins. This will allow you to see where you've been and take a good look ahead.

Once you have dates mapped out for holidays and promotions, much of your Quarterly Content Plan may be filled in already. You'll be left with some empty spots that you'll fill with content that meets the needs of your Beginner, Intermediate, and Advanced audience members. We'll do that in the next step.

MONTHLY CONTENT PLAN: HELP YOUR BUSINESS AND YOUR AUDIENCE

SHIFT YOUR MINDSET TO BIG

Before you dive into creating your Monthly Content Plan, I want to encourage you to think BIG. Here's the question I want you to ask yourself:

> *If my website was the most respected resource in the world on my topic, what information would it share? How would the information be presented?*

If your product or service was the very first answer to the question "Who's the best on this topic?" what would your content strategy be?

I realize this may be a little overwhelming, and you may not be able to position your site as the number one resource right away — or ever.

But I urge you to think big when thinking about your content. You're not just churning out ideas here — you're building a business. Hold fast to a vision of how your content will position your website at the top of your industry.

Don't aim to be one of a crowd — aim to be the best.

Your Monthly Content Plan is the place where you'll get granular — you'll plan your content week by week. In the Monthly Content Plan, you will:

- Note the topics you'll cover with specific pieces of content
- Plan which category or categories you expect to file each piece under
- Do initial research about the keyword phrases you'll target
- Make notes about how you'll promote each piece once it's published

Mapping out these details ahead of time means you won't sit down to write with a blank page — and a blank look on your face! You'll have goals and the beginnings of a plan that will help you reach them.

How does existing content fit into your future plans?

What if you have already published some content — maybe *a lot* of content? How will existing content fit into your month-by-month content plan?

Take stock of the content assets you already have. Review your current content and take your data into account.

Data-Driven Method. In Chapter 5, we talked about using analytics data to direct your maintenance tasks around the most-visited pieces on a mature site. That data can also be used to revive existing content that was well-received the first time and suits your goals now.

You'll log in to Google Analytics and perform the same search we talked about earlier. In the left column, select Behavior. Under that, choose Site Content. And under that, choose All Pages. Following this sequence will tell Google Analytics to serve up a list of your most-visited pages.

Make a list of your top 50 pages in order from most-visited to least. Are there any pieces of existing content that will help move your business closer to its goals? Highlight the content that is a perfect fit, and make notes about pages to update.

The Archaeology Method. This is a more hands-on method. You're going to delve into your archives to look for hidden gems.

As you skim their titles, do you spot some content that deserves to come back around to front and center because it is a perfect fit for your goals? Maybe it never got the attention it deserved when it was first published, and you want to give it a second chance. Sometimes this happens if your content is published on a busy news day, or if you release it during a time that many people are on vacation.

Make a list of this content and make notes about what to polish up and weave into your Monthly Content Plan. It might be easiest to do this on a spreadsheet. More on this in the next chapter.

And yes, it's perfectly fine to make updates to existing content! Since others may have linked to it, it's important to not change the underlying premise or the permalink. But adding information, making small modifications, and deleting anything that makes the piece seem outdated can help breathe new life into old content.

If you have a mature site, you'll want to budget some time to do this content maintenance work alongside your weekly content creation tasks, not only to prepare for promotions. For more, review "Your Maintenance Tasks in Order of Importance" in Chapter 5.

CHECKLIST | PLAN YEARLY, QUARTERLY, AND MONTHLY CONTENT

Your content plan will grow, change, and evolve as time goes by. Think about your big goals, map out how you'll reach them, and make specific plans that guide your day-to-day work.

- Create a Yearly Content Plan that's a broad overview of your business goals and includes a vision for the year ahead
- Map out a Quarterly Content Plan that adds dates for promotions and holidays, and work your content around those
- Make a Monthly Content Plan that you'll use to guide your week-by-week content creation.

It's not always easy to carve out time to do this kind of long-term thinking that leads to solid action plans that guide your day-to-day work and point directly at your goals — but it's worth it!

MAKING YOUR CONTENT STRATEGY REAL

My dream for you as we wrap up this book is that you leave with a plan you can implement — a boots-on-the-ground map you'll follow as you create content week by week and month by month.

For this to happen, we need to take the ideas embodied in this book and put them into a visible format you can follow. And to find a format you'll love using, I'd like you to decide between the two descriptors below, so I can recommend the format that you'll enjoy using most.

When it comes to planning, are you a person who:

Enjoys using online tools like apps, websites, and checklists that you can easily access from your computer and your phone? Do you value the ability to jump in and add ideas or edit plans from anywhere? If so, you're an *App Appreciator.*

Or are you a person who:

Prefers a plan you can touch and interact with in the real world, like a notebook, a whiteboard, or a large piece of paper with sticky notes you can move around? Do you value touch, writing, and physically interacting with your information? If so, you're a *Tangible Planner.*

Some people are a little bit of both of these descriptors! That's me — and if that's you, too, read about the solutions here and choose one that's a happy combination of both approaches.

WHAT SHOULD YOU INCLUDE IN YOUR VISIBLE CONTENT STRATEGY?

Let's review the information you'll include in your visible content strategy, no matter how you capture it.

As a starting point, you'll want to have an idea of your target **publishing frequency.** How often will you publish new content? For more on this, go back to Part I and read about the lifecycle approach to content strategy in Chapter 1.

You'll need a place to add the **content topic** — remember, you'll work on the headline as part of your 4-Day Content Creation System. At this point, just note the subject or theme.

You'll want to add your **publishing date,** so you can work backward from it and start creating the content with plenty of time to spare.

If there's space in your plan, you can add information about the **call to action** you'll include.

You could add more information like: the **category** you'll assign; the **author,** if you publish a multi-author website; the **link** to the final product; or anything else you want to track on an ongoing basis.

I know you're busy, so start with the basics! The idea here is to create a visible content strategy to guide you — not to create a document that becomes a burden to maintain. A real-life content strategy is an essential last step in this process. It will be your guide for the journey, so it should be easy for you to create, follow, and edit as needed.

Here's what your content strategy should include, at a minimum:

- Your target **publishing frequency**
- Your **content topic**
- Your **publishing date**

LET'S GET VISIBLE

For the App Appreciator

Spreadsheet software. I really love spreadsheet software for mapping out a content strategy. Google Spreadsheets works great, and it lets you add advanced options like checkboxes and conditional formatting, which can help you organize your content strategy as it grows.

Trello. Trello fans are visual thinkers who enjoy the flexibility of a solution that allows them to combine checklists, due dates, task assignments, links, text, and images for each piece of content they make a card for.

Mind mapping software. For the non-linear thinker, mind mapping software makes it easy to capture ideas, add to them, and rearrange them. There are many options — MindMeister is cross-platform compatible and cloud-based, and it is a good place to start.

No matter which software tool you use, you'll appreciate the ability to see your planned content on a calendar. More on that in the "Ultimate Commitment" section ahead.

FOR THE TANGIBLE PLANNER

A notebook and a pencil. People who love notebooks *really* love notebooks. To use a notebook for content planning, I recommend investing in a three-ring binder and tabbed dividers. You can use the dividers any way you'd like, but one place to start would be a section for content ideas and another for your planned content. Write these plans in pencil so you can easily change them as needed. The rings will allow you to pop open the binder and move pages around when — not if — your content plans evolve.

A whiteboard. Whiteboards give you plenty of space to spread out and think big. If you have access to one and can leave your plan up for a while, this can be a good place to map out your content before you add it to a calendar. Use different colors to indicate different information.

A large piece of paper with sticky notes. No whiteboard? Try a large piece of white paper as a foundation for your content plan. I'm partial to those oversized sticky notes that come on an easel. They can be torn off the pad and stuck to a wall. Whatever you use, combining large paper and a pad of smaller sticky notes gives you a flexible way to map out your plan. The smaller notes can be used to write down your content topic and planned publishing date.

THE ULTIMATE COMMITMENT: ASSIGNING DATES TO YOUR PLAN

The final step to making your content strategy visible is to note your plans on your favorite calendar. As mentioned in Chapter 11, it's smart to think ahead to promotions you have planned and offers you'll make. This will allow you to create a content strategy that:

- Directs your audience's attention to the topic of your offer
- Builds anticipation for the solution you've built

- Answers questions they may have about your offer or solution
- Builds an email list of interested prospects (if this is a business goal)

There are a couple of ways to assign dates to a calendar, and they mirror our two descriptors mentioned above.

FOR THE APP APPRECIATOR

The Editorial Calendar plugin. If you're on WordPress, you're in luck. The Editorial Calendar plugin is a super simple — but powerful — content planner. It allows you to add content to dates and, as you do that, create WordPress draft posts that are ready to edit.

A digital calendar. You can use your Google, iCal, or Outlook calendar as a content planner, too. Consider creating a dedicated calendar with its own color for content planning, so it's easy to spot among your appointments.

FOR THE TANGIBLE PLANNER

A paper calendar and a pencil. Tangible Planners, rejoice! A blank calendar and a pencil give you the ultimate flexible system for mapping out content. If something changes, simply erase, move, and rewrite.

A whiteboard-style calendar. If you're a fan of whiteboards, you can purchase a large calendar to pin on your wall and use it to assign dates to the content you'll create.

NO MATTER WHICH TOOL YOU USE, BE SURE THAT MAKING edits and changes is simple. Content strategy is never written in stone, and the more flexible your system, the easier you'll find it to use.

CHECKLIST | MAKING YOUR CONTENT STRATEGY REAL

Committing your content strategy to a visible format you can easily follow means you can avoid sitting in front of your screen wondering what content you need to create this week. Make your plan, and work that plan!

- Commit your content strategy to a format that feels comfortable and easy for you
- At a minimum, be sure your content strategy includes your publishing frequency, content topics, and publishing dates
- Weave in promotional plans, if you have them, so you can use content during the warm-up and launch periods

Pick a format you'll enjoy using and get your strategy mapped out so you have a plan to follow for the boots-on-the-ground phase of your content journey.

18

A LAST WORD: THE CONTENT MARKETER'S MINDSET

I BELIEVE THAT MASTERING CONTENT MARKETING CAN HELP you grow as a person and a business owner in interesting and unexpected ways.

First off, it's an opportunity to "practice in public." In the early years of content creation, hitting publish can be a nausea-inducing moment. At a time when you don't feel 100% confident about your abilities, you're putting your work out into the world. Here's a news flash:

> *Every successful content creator experienced this in their early years. You know what they did? They felt that uncomfortable feeling and hit publish anyway.*

As you create content, over time, your skills increase and so does your comfort level. You step fully into your role as a publisher — one whose content expertise and confidence shine.

Practicing your content creation skills in public might be nerve-wracking, but remember: You have important information to share, and the only way to find the people who need it is to hit publish.

Content marketing is my favorite example of a creative task that is good for business. Embrace the ever-growing complexity of your content marketing tasks as a way to build your creative chops *and* your business.

And now, to answer a question I hear a lot…

"DO I HAVE TO HAVE A PERFECT PLAN BEFORE I START CREATING CONTENT?"

You don't. Many, many high-impact websites do little planning and, instead, opt for a "fly by the seat of your pants" method that works well for them.

You can do that if you choose. If your website creates content that responds to current news, industry trends, or cultural happenings, that might be the perfect approach.

But if you're a more traditional online business owner who's using content marketing to build an audience for your products and services, you may find yourself craving some kind of map to follow. That's what this book will help you build.

> *Creating your content with clear goals in mind means that what you produce will have a better chance of moving you closer to those goals.*

But there's a danger here — some people get caught up in creating the perfect plan. They think they can't move forward until they've mapped out every step of the journey ahead of time.

Don't let your *planning* take the place of your *creating*.

Remember that, in the end, you must create. Your content won't help your business if you only plan it, but don't actually publish it.

At some point, you have to forge ahead with your content, whether your plan is ready to go or not.

The content you publish will work for your business only when it's live, searchable, and consumable. Plus, the only way to begin gathering data about what works — or doesn't work — is to publish and see what happens.

Think about the business transformation you want to achieve with your content — and the transformation you want to deliver to your audience. Build your new content around those and use your older content to reinforce your efforts.

Need extra help? Get free *Master Content Strategy* bonus materials at MasterContentStrategy.com/bonus

19

I WISH YOU JOY ON YOUR JOURNEY

WE LIVE IN AN AWE-INSPIRING TIME, WHEN ONE PERSON IN front of a lightweight piece of metal and plastic can influence hundreds of thousands of other people across the world. I hope you'll see this moment in time for what it is — *a miracle.*

This miracle can help you grow as a person, and it can help your business reach well beyond your geographic borders to find the exact right people you wish to serve, no matter where they live.

I hope this book makes your journey feel doable, fun, and inspiring.

Read on for smart advice from some of the most successful content marketers I know. They all started as beginners, and they have generously shared insights from their years of experience.

20
CONTENT MARKETERS TALK STRATEGY

As I considered how to teach content strategy, I looked to some of the smartest content marketers I know for inspiration. These content marketers have mature websites, so they have been through all the phases of the website lifecycle and come out the other side.

And before I finished writing this book, I reached out to ask if they'd share their hard-earned lessons with you.

There are some golden nuggets of wisdom in the pages ahead! Enjoy learning from these experienced content marketers. My deepest gratitude to:

- **Jeff Brown** of Read to Lead Podcast
- **Douglas Burdett** of Artillery Marketing
- **Andy Crestodina** of Orbit Media
- **Dave Delaney** of Future Forth
- **Sean D'Souza** of Psychotactics

- **Henneke Duistermaat** of Enchanting Marketing
- **Kerry O'Shea Gorgone** of MarketingProfs
- **Karyn Greenstreet** of Passion for Business
- **John Jantsch** of Duct Tape Marketing
- **Chris Lema** of Liquid Web
- **Sean McCabe** of SeanWes
- **Angus Nelson** of AngusNelson.com
- **Joanna Penn** of The Creative Penn
- **Jeff Sanders** of JeffSanders.com
- **Mark Schaefer** of Businesses Grow
- **Andrea Vahl** of AndreaVahl.com
- **Joanna Wiebe** of Copyhackers

"WHAT HARD-EARNED LESSON HAVE YOU DISCOVERED ABOUT CONTENT STRATEGY THAT YOU'D LIKE TO SHARE?"

The answers to the question above are as varied as the people who answered! They all contain great wisdom. Some are surprising — and some are quite contrarian.

Andy Crestodina says to ignore tactics and focus on creating a solid, measurable strategy instead.

"Strategic thinking in digital is surprisingly rare. There are so many channels and tools that it's easy to get lured in by a tactic or idea ... and lose sight of the audience or business goals. This is common.

Less common but also tragic is a good idea or action (focused on both audience needs and business goals) that isn't measured. The thinking was strategic, but the impact isn't measured and opportunities for ongoing optimization are missed.

Every idea is a hypothesis and every action is a test. This is how the best content strategists think."

Joanna Wiebe says editorial calendars are overrated — and can stifle creativity.

"The biggest lesson is that an editorial calendar is usually far more the friend of the project manager than of the actual content creator.

It's nice to have a plan to follow, sure, with topics and when to have 'em done by. But the reality is that, when you're creating really powerful content, an editorial calendar can actually get in the way of one's best work. The best content we've seen — measured in terms of organic traffic, comments and social shares — is the content that we were triggered **by real life** *to create.*

We learned this lesson during a month-long exercise in which five key members of our team wrote one post a week for a month (for a total of twenty posts); in the end, the only post that got **any** *traffic was the one written based on a real pain I'd been going through for about six months.*

And it got a **ton** *of traffic. The spike was crazy. So we have to ask ourselves — were the other 19 posts a good investment of time and energy for our team? And the answer to that question, a year later, is not what I would've hoped a year ago.*

The posts that perform best for us are, consistently, the ones driven by what's actually happening to us in X moment. I've never found an editorial calendar, with its focus on writing, say, keyword-rich 800-word posts, to actually lead to the business results we're told it'll get us. Don't get me wrong — I think you can guide creativity. But I don't think editorial calendars actually do that. They create content factories, in my experience. And no one cares about content that's been churned out of a machine.

The flip side of this — the thing that makes this lesson particularly hard *to learn — is that, when you follow an editorial calendar, you actually get sh*t done. So there's that."*

Chris Lema advocates for writing using the everyday language your audience is using — or risk losing the people who don't know the right words to use.

"I don't know if you've ever gone to Google to look for something, only to realize that you don't even know the exact words to use to get the right results. But it happens to me all the time. My wife, one time, in an effort to make sure she didn't look up kids movie times for a date we were going on, typed 'adult movies' into Google. Trust me, that wasn't what she wanted.

So the lesson I have learned about content strategy is that we often focus on keywords, long-tail search phrases and all sorts of ways to make sure our content connects with people who know what to ask for. But we often skip writing content for people who don't yet know the problem vocabulary. If you're building a bunk bed for your kids, you may know you need a new piece of equipment, but there's a good chance you don't know what it's called.

This is a case of being so familiar with a subject that we have to step away to create content topics for those that come from outside the space and need to learn the problem vocabulary before they can be introduced to the solution vocabulary."

For **Henneke Duistermaat,** staying open to new ideas has been a key to her success with content marketing.

"My main lesson has been to experiment. As a traditionally schooled marketer, I learned to plan every marketing campaign beforehand, but I've found that when I'm open to ideas, listen to my readers and experiment, my strategy may shift direction and my content gets better, resonating more strongly with my audience.

For instance, I used to write mainly about copywriting and blogging techniques. But when I tried writing more personal posts about procrastination and self-doubts, I discovered that many in my audience were struggling with the same issues. Such posts resonated with my audience and helped me bond — they've become a key part of my positioning. I wouldn't have discovered that without experimentation."

Andrea Vahl urges you to be prepared to put in the time — but to look forward to the payoff, too.

"Writing good blog posts takes time. I can sometimes spend six hours on a blog post. But when you have good content, your site gets a lot of traffic and you can leverage that into leads and sales."

Kerry O'Shea Gorgone has some tough love for us.

"No one cares about you, your brand, or your company.

That's a tough one to swallow, but it's a fact.

No one cares about your content, either, unless and until your content is relevant and helpful to them. If you want to succeed in marketing and in business, frame every touchpoint (content, customer service, sales) around the customer's needs and wants. Many marketers seem to know this, but they haven't taken the lesson to heart. If they had, we'd see much less "sales-y" content out there!"

Douglas Burdett shares a gentle reminder that it all starts with staying in touch with what your site visitors are searching for.

"Regardless of the content topic, the more you can address your audience's latent desires or anxieties, the more likely it will resonate."

Mark Schaefer is here with his best recommendations to avoid contributing to content overload.

"Content strategy does not begin with content. It begins with research.

Producing content is a big commitment, so before you just dive in, stand back, assess your marketplace to discover:

- *How much information density exists for your topical niche? Do you have a chance to compete?*
- *Where are your competitors dominating? Where are the open niches?*
- *What is the best way to maneuver in your competitive environment in a way that can produce sustainable results?*

The number one problem today (by far) is that businesses produce content that simply contributes to the noise. Spend time upfront thinking about how you will break free of that."

Jeff Sanders says your enthusiasm around your topic speaks louder than words.

"Curiosity may be your most powerful tool. When you are passionate, inquisitive, and fascinated about learning as much as you can about your content, you invest more time, energy, and enthusiasm into discovering and sharing your best and brightest insights.

Your audience will easily recognize your genuine curiosity and then naturally find themselves leaning in to learn more as well. Likewise, if you lose interest in your content or become jaded over time, your audience can easily detect that too.

Let your own genuine curiosity guide you as you explore more about your area of expertise — it will serve you and your tribe like nothing else can."

And finally, **Jeff Brown** reminds us that showing up — consistently — is the most important thing you can do.

"I have found that consistency is key to any content marketing strategy.

Most marketers will at some point ask me some variation of "How often should I publish my content?" That's the wrong question to ask.

The frequency at which you publish content is far less important than most people realize. Just don't bite off more than you can chew. Simply choose a content schedule you're confident you can keep up with.

Just by showing up on a regular basis, you will put yourself ahead of most other marketers.

Your audience will feel you're someone they can count on. You will build trust with them more quickly.

Put simply, consistency trumps everything!"

"HOW FAR IN ADVANCE DO YOU PLAN THE CONTENT YOU'LL PUBLISH?"

Do the smartest content marketers fly by the seat of their pants? Do they wait for inspiration to strike? Or do they map everything out ahead of time? The answers vary — and they're often a combination of all of the above.

Mark Schaefer's Businesses Grow site is all about commentary on the here and now. So planning too far in advance doesn't work for him.

"I only plan my content a week or so in advance and the reason is simple: I provide commentary and ideas based on what is new, and now, and changing. I am normally the first person in my industry to do so. This provides a competitive advantage because people like to share content and ideas that are fresh. The top sharers are 'new junkies!'

If I were wedded to a content calendar, I would just be like everybody else."

By contrast, **Kerry O'Shea Gorgone** juggles not just her own schedule but also that of the many guests she interviews on the

MarketingProfs podcast. So mapping out content in advance is crucial.

"The MarketingProfs podcast, Marketing Smarts, is planned several months in advance. I do shuffle things around a bit, but we need some kind of production schedule in order to balance topics, guest backgrounds, and industries."

Andrea Vahl keeps a content idea library — a topic I covered in *Master Content Marketing.*

"A lot of times I'm picking from a list that I've written of possible topics. But if I have a launch, I will plan the posts each week leading up to that launch to help draw the audience into that topic.

Occasionally there is a big change or breaking news that I want to cover. That can lead to a big spike in traffic but I don't just cover the "facts" of the breaking news, I let people know how it will impact them and how they should change their outlook."

Henneke Duistermaat's trusty paper notebook supplies her best ideas.

"I don't plan a lot in advance. I have a notebook (an old-fashioned paper one!) where I scribble down ideas for new posts, so I always have plenty of ideas to choose from.

I publish blog posts every other week, and I pick an idea from my notebook about 5 days in advance. I write and edit my post over a series of days, working in small chunks of time.

I am a relatively low social media user as I prioritize blog writing. I am most active on Twitter and schedule my tweets one to three days in advance. Especially if you're a solopreneur, it's important to set priorities. I'd rather do a few activities well."

Joanna Wiebe surges forward when she has an idea that lights her (and her team) up.

"Once we get a good idea — one where we're like, "Oh I'd love to read that/take that quiz/watch that tutorial," we give ourselves about three weeks to get it published."

And **Andy Crestodina** nurtures the seeds of his content ideas until they're ready to grow into full-blown articles.

"There is a list with dozens of ideas and partially written articles. They are like seeds that grow when I add new ideas and examples to them. If I spot a piece of research or example that relates to one of these, I capture it and that potential article grows. They sometimes stay in this state for months or years, slowing growing.

Then a few weeks before I have an article due (our newsletter is bi-weekly), I start going through this list and look for something that I could shape into a finished piece. I pick one that supports a theme I'm working on and dig in.

I'll spend six-eight hours over the next ten days writing, re-writing, preparing images, asking experts for contributor quotes and polishing. Three days before it launches, it goes to Amanda for editing, final image prep and writing a bunch of possible headline and subject lines."

"WHAT TOOLS OR TECHNIQUES HAVE YOU FOUND WORK REALLY WELL FOR MAPPING OUT YOUR CONTENT STRATEGY?"

If you think you're going to get a bunch of software solutions here, think again. These content marketers propose everything from whiteboards to a philosophy of working ahead.

Sean McCabe highly recommends the peace of mind you'll get from developing a "content buffer."

"It is a huge commitment to post consistently and stay on track. It takes a lot of discipline.

Resist the urge to publish content as soon as you've finished it. Instead, get ahead and create a buffer for yourself. Stack up some finished content in a queue that is scheduled to publish ahead of time.

For weekly output, I recommend having a four to six-week buffer. This means you have four to six pieces of completed content scheduled and ready to go in advance.

For daily output, I recommend having a 10- to 14-day buffer or 10 to 14 pieces of completed content scheduled and ready to go in advance.

Before you start publishing weekly or daily, build up a queue of content. Prove to yourself that you're going to be serious by creating a buffer of content before you publish the first piece.

If you don't create a content buffer, you will eventually fall off.

Break the habit of finishing things the night before they are due by getting ahead."

Andy Crestodina has a one-word solution for mapping out content strategy.

"Whiteboards!"

Sean D'Souza uses advanced planning and content buffers to take extensive time off every year.

"We take three months off every year.

This means that we have to plan well in advance, right? Not necessarily. Often an article is pretty much touch and go. Or at least it used to be in the past. I would be writing them on a weekly basis and just in time for the deadline (which isn't much different from a news reporter). However, as we reach the time to go off on another trip, we have to be more vigilant (and often more productive).

This means that we have to queue newsletters in advance, but not just for the four weeks that we're away but also for at least four to six weeks after we return. This means we can have a decent reentry and not have to rush to write new content. This applies to podcasts as well as newsletters to 5000bc (our membership site) and Psychotactics itself.

Over time, I found that writing longer articles help. Today I routinely write articles that are about 4,000-5,000 words long and that enables us to break them up into three parts (sometimes) and so we get greater mileage out of a single article. I still write four to five articles a month, but now they are able to be broken up and they go for fifteen weeks instead of four to five weeks. That's kept our nose above water. It's an evolving strategy."

Angus Nelson recommends the "waterfall" approach to create multiple pieces of content from one single effort.

"Creating an abundance of great content can be really challenging. However, if you build your content to waterfall into additional iterations of the same content, you'll discover more with less.

For instance, you can shoot a video of an interview or presentation first. This one piece of content can then be multiplied into a dozen other pieces — the video can be edited into multiple, individual snippets. You can also take out images and add text with quotes as a quote card. Then you can strip out the audio for a podcast, sound bytes, testimonials, or audiograms. Then, the audio can be transcribed and used in an ebook, white paper, or a chapter in a book.

*The more you think **waterfall**, the more quality content you can create."*

Karyn Greenstreet looks at her promotion plans and maps out her content accordingly.

"I work backwards from the goal. And the goals can change, based on my marketing plan for that quarter. If I'm promoting a specific class

that quarter, then all content is geared towards the class topic and designed/paced in such a way to lead the reader to a conclusion.

*For instance, if I'm teaching a class about how to design a lesson plan, each piece of content for the quarter will give tips and advice about how to do it and why it's important to have a lesson plan. The content will include practical guidance, inspiration success stories, pitfalls and road bumps they'll encounter — all to encourage people to decide that lesson plans **are** important and that they can't wait to learn more and master the topic themselves!"*

Kerry O'Shea Gorgone goes straight for the sticky notes for maximum flexibility when planning.

"For early conceptual planning, nothing works better for me than sticky notes! (Seriously.) I need to be able to rough out a strategy, then move pieces around or discard them altogether.

There are definitely digital tools I could use for this, but there's something about writing goals and tactics down and physically handling the notes that help the strategy to gel in my mind."

Joanna Wiebe uses a simple spreadsheet to see her content in a single glance.

"A Google sheet. We have a calendar in our Google sheet, and we just populate the cells with the topic, the writer and important dates: when the editor will see it, when I'll see it, when we hope to publish it, when we'll send the email about it.

We keep it simple and streamlined.

Our social media lives outside our primary content strategy — because creation and distribution, although tied, each require really unique and concentrated strategies and tactics, in our experience."

"WHAT ARE THE MOST IMPORTANT CONSIDERATIONS PEOPLE SHOULD KEEP IN MIND AS THEY PLAN THEIR CONTENT STRATEGY?"

Priorities vary in this group of answers. But each thoughtful sentence is the product of years of experience.

For **Dave Delaney**, the three Rs come to mind.

"When I ran social media and content marketing for a popular consumer electronics company, I wrote and published five blog posts per week. Those blog posts were in addition to the email newsletters, affiliate relations, social networking, and sweepstakes on my plate each week.

*My solution was something I help many of my clients with today, it's based on a phrase you may be familiar with: Reuse, Reduce, Recycle. I mastered the ability to **reuse** popular content and **recycle** it into new forms of content (such as videos, images, long-form posts, short-form posts, infographics). Doing this would greatly **reduce** my stress of having to come up with new content each day."*

Andy Crestodina recommends you show your ego to the door and focus on the facts.

"Marketers have opinions and egos, like everyone else. We like this and don't like that.

But our personal preferences are not reason enough to make marketing decisions. The marketers who can overcome their own biases get the best results. They add their opinions and ideas to a long list of many hypotheses. Then they prioritize the possible options before taking action.

There's all kinds of room for creativity, but without a large set of ideas you can't prioritize, test, measure and improve!"

John Jantsch reminds you to ask yourself some crucial questions before you produce a new piece of content.

"I think every piece of content should be mapped to your customer journey — it forces you to ask why you are producing it. You need content for awareness and trust building and that's probably not the same content an engaged buyer needs."

Douglas Burdett seconds the observation above.

"Two things: the buyer persona and their buyer's journey. Each piece of content needs to answer which persona it is for and which point in their journey the content addresses."

Henneke Duistermaat reminds us that we're not preaching — we're conversing.

"Content is not a monologue, it's a two-way conversation with readers, listeners and viewers. When planning your strategy, it's important to think about both sides of your conversation:

A. Your audience

What are your readers interested in learning? How can you help them? Which problems can you help solve?

When you let go of the idea of selling, and instead position yourself as a mentor to your readers, you build your authority naturally, and readers will come to you for advice.

B. You (as content creator)

What are you excited about? What would you love to write about?

Readers sense the enthusiasm in your writing; it's contagious. So, the best content is at the sweet spot of what excites you as creator and what your audience is keen to learn.

You may find you're more excited when you share not just your existing knowledge, but also what you're discovering and learning. My blog, for instance, reflects my own journey of learning how to write better. I keep exploring.

If you're writing about a seemingly boring topic for clients, try to find experts and talk to them — let their enthusiasm inspire you.

Remember to have fun."

Kerry O'Shea Gorgone brings hard-earned wisdom from managing multiple content contributors.

"You must structure your content plan to avoid burning out your top contributors. So often, people overburden their top performers because their work is so good. Eventually, even the highest capacity employees will buckle under a massive workload! Pace yourself, spread the work around, and create a strategy that takes your resources (financial and human) into consideration."

Angus Nelson says to look for a way to intersect with your audience's needs and emotions.

*"Create your content with the intent to **intersect**, not **interrupt**. So much content today is little more than blasts of force-fed content promoting someone's product or service. This kind of "look at me" content is a blatant interruption to someone's day and life.*

*However, if you create content that speaks to how a service or product adds value, relieves a pain, or brings a solution — then you have something people connect to and **feel**. It's at the intersection of your audience's needs and emotions that they make decisions."*

Mark Schaefer reminds us that consumers have the power today — and we would do well to be of service with our content.

"You need to adopt a mindset of today's hyper-empowered consumer. The purpose of your content is not to insert a person into a slot in your "sales funnel."

Content serves as a data point in their customer journey, which is maddeningly complex. That journey must depend on trust first and foremost, not a promise of being spammed because they downloaded an article. Use content to build trust, not to destroy it."

Jeff Sanders is a proponent of … *under*planning? Read on to learn his logic for this recommendation.

"Less is more when it comes to the quantity of content you plan to produce. Seriously under-plan the number of blog posts, podcast episodes, video series, and products you plan to release. The biggest mistake I see with any new content creator is getting overly ambitious when they first start out.

In podcasting, there is a phenomenon known as "podfading," releasing fewer episodes over time until eventually the podcast no longer produces anything at all. I launched my podcast with the goal of only one new episode per week and I stuck to that for over four years (234 episodes in a row). Consistency like this is nearly unheard of in any medium because consistency is seriously hard work.

As counter-intuitive as it may seem, setting a seemingly low bar and hitting it every time is the difference maker between those who succeed long-term and those who explode out of the gate, but then inevitably fade away, never to be heard from again."

And finally, **Joanna Wiebe** reminds us that our content strategy is a living organism — and so are we!

"The best bloggers need major downtime! We're like deep-sea divers — you can't expect us to plunge all the way down to the bottom of the ocean to reveal things no one's ever seen or heard before … come up for air … and head straight back down. We need recovery time. So consider the likelihood of major creation fatigue for your regular contributors; have a roster of freelancers at the ready to write the non-cornerstone pieces while your top talent is recovering.

Also keep in mind the need for flexibility. A timely post based on what's going on now, seen through your brand's lens, is more likely to get shared on FB than an old post about best practices. So build flexibility and responsiveness into your plan.

If you don't know what to write about, don't write. This is different from writing novels, etc., where the rule is to write even when you don't want to.

Brian Clark first said to me, "Everything is content." Those three words have been huge in shaping how I publish and what I write. So with your strategy, build in opportunities to turn unexpected stuff that's happening every day for you — like how your business does X and why hiring Y was so hard for you — into content.

*Lastly, in my opinion, is this: make your content strategy a living document. It will change. It **should** change. If it doesn't change, it's probably not relevant."*

"HOW HAS YOUR APPROACH TO CONTENT STRATEGY EVOLVED OVER THE YEARS? WHAT ARE YOU BETTER AT NOW THAN YOU WERE BEFORE?"

I find it incredibly comforting to realize that even experienced, admired content marketers were once beginners. With this question, we hear what the years have taught them.

Joanna Wiebe has come to realize that there are no hard-and-fast rules that last forever when it comes to using content marketing in her business.

"I'm better at cutting myself and my team some slack! That doesn't mean you're allowed to miss a deadline, of course.

I'm worse at committing to a vision. If anything, that's where I personally need the most help as a content creator and publisher. We've switched between "let's publish 4x a month" to "let's publish only when we're excited" and back again about 700 times."

Compared to the early days, **John Jantsch** now uses a more thoughtful approach to the content he creates.

"Initially I was a blogger — I often wrote for myself more than my business objectives. That was the right thing to do in 2005, but today everything I produce goes into an annual plan to create content that drives goals for SEO, lead generation and conversion. I like to think it's probably more useful too."

Henneke Duistermaat has found that writing about "teeny-tiny topics" helps a lot. And learning a new, exciting skill that contributes to her site's personality has made a big difference!

"When you're writing a blog for a number of years, it can be tough to keep going. Two tactics have kept me excited about blogging.

Firstly, to narrow the topics of blog posts. I regularly write about teeny-tiny topics such as how to write an opening line or how to use adverbs. Writing about a mix of tiny and big topics has helped me grow my search traffic.

Secondly, to explore topics on the edge of my topic. My core expertise is copywriting and blog writing, but over the years, I've been blogging about self-care for writers, storytelling and creativity, too.

Another exciting change for me has been learning to draw. I hadn't drawn since I'd been at school, so learning to draw and publishing my simple illustrations on my blog was a big step for me.

I find that the two creative skills — writing and drawing — feed off each other. Drawing helps me come up with metaphors for blog posts, and when I'm stuck writing, I draw."

Andrea Vahl knows how to hook readers and keep them on the line.

"I am better at writing headlines and opening hooks than before. I also write answers to questions that I answer over and over so I can refer people to that post. That makes me more efficient when helping people."

Kerry O'Shea Gorgone has become choosy about where she shows up online.

"As more and more social networks and channels become available, I've tended to become more strategic about which platforms I use. When there were only a few to worry about, it was easier to maintain a presence "everywhere" (or, at least, everywhere that mattered to your audience). Now that being everywhere is truly impossible, I've been forced to critically examine the various channels and platforms to determine where my audience is, then focus my efforts there."

For **Joanna Penn,** juggling content creation with the life of a prolific author has given her multiple new learning experiences.

"My strategy for TheCreativePenn.com has always been to consistently share useful and inspiring articles, podcasts, and videos about my lessons learned about writing, publishing, book marketing and making a living with my writing. I started the site to share my own journey and after 10 years of putting out content every 2-3 days, I still have so much to share. My keywords and search engine optimization have emerged from being clear about my niche and my target audience continues to be people like me — those who want to see their books out in the world.

I learned about SEO headlines from Copyblogger early on and this has made a big difference in terms of the content that continues to be found — writing books is very different to writing copy.

I use Google Sheets to plan my content, sharing the document with my virtual assistant who manages guest posts and also the transcripts for my podcast. My podcast interviews are planned three to six months in advance, but I also do YouTube videos every week which I decide on just prior to recording and I change my blog posts regularly, depending on feedback from my audience and what is happening in the independent author community."

Jeff Sanders finds that content creation has given him the space to expand creatively like nothing else has.

"There is a slogan in long-distance running that says, "you are stronger than you think you are, and you can do more than you think you can." This is true in content creation as well.

We are all so much stronger, smarter, and savvier than we believe inside our doubt-filled minds. Content creation is hard, no doubt, but we have more tools, resources, experience, and ingenuity than we need to continually produce amazing content for the rest of our lives.

Over time, I have proven to myself again and again that I have what it takes to be the rock star I once dreamed I could become, and I have an obligation to share my thoughts, insights, and experiences with others. They can learn from me, and I owe it to them to give my best every time."

Andy Crestodina pays attention to the numbers — and has seen his website grow year after year as a result. But it sounds like he misses some of the old days, too.

"The more I measure results, the more I narrow in on the topics and formats that perform well. This means better results year over year and steady increases in traffic and leads.

But sometimes I miss the old days. In the early years, I did a lot more experimental content. One post was a poem. Another was a crossword puzzle.

So I've gotten better at driving results by focusing on what performs well, but it may be time to break out and try some crazy new ideas and inject some chaos into my dataset!"

"ANYTHING ELSE YOU'D LIKE TO ADD?"

Andrea Vahl gets the last word — and it's a word of encouragement for all of us!

"Don't let anyone tell you that blogging is dead. Content and sharing your philosophy is what draws potential clients to you. It's how I got my book deal and it's how I get a lot of speaking engagements — because my site ranks for keywords.

Also, make sure you add in some of your personal story every once in a while if you can. People want to learn about you and get to know the person behind the content."

MAY I ASK YOU FOR A SMALL FAVOR?

Thank you for making the time to read this entire book. I hope it becomes your go-to planning tool for creating content that makes a BIG impact in your online business.

If you enjoyed reading *Master Content Strategy*, would you be willing to let others know what you thought about it? There are several ways to do this. You could:

- Add your review to Amazon.com
- Write a review on Goodreads.com
- Share the book with your audience in your content or an email
- Mention *Master Content Strategy* on social media
- Talk about the book with your colleagues and friends

Any of these actions makes a huge difference to an author like me! They're your vote of confidence in my work, and I truly appreciate your support. Thank you.

– PAMELA WILSON

APPENDIX

In this appendix, you'll find all the checklists I added to the end of the chapters that form the heart of this book. They cover how to map out a content strategy that maximizes your reach and boosts your bottom line every time you publish.

Here's my best advice at a glance:

THE THREE LIFECYCLE STAGES: A BRIEF OVERVIEW

Your approach to raising your profile using content marketing is going to morph through the years. This book helped you anticipate and plan the work you'll do in each stage of your website's growth.

Here are the three lifecycle stages:

YOUR NEW WEBSITE: BIRTH THROUGH YEAR 1

On a brand-new website, you'll focus on populating your pages with helpful content that establishes your expertise.

Aim for:

A new piece every week, so by the end of the first year, you'll have become an experienced content creator *and* filled your website's pages with content you'll link to and from for years to come.

Clear, consistent categories, so people arriving on your website understand who it's for and what it offers.

Polished content that makes a great impression. Aim to hone your voice and to get better with every piece you publish.

YOUR GROWING WEBSITE: YEAR 2 THROUGH YEAR 5

Your website is still new at this stage, and now you will have some flesh-and-blood audience members. You can do things like ask them to leave a response in your comments section or on social media. You can create content to help with their real-life challenges.

Aim for:

A new piece at least every other week, so you can continue to serve up useful, engaging information your audience can count on.

Deep-dive content that delivers in-depth information on specific topics that help your audience and your business.

Multimedia content that expands your message to other plat-forms. If you haven't explored repurposing your content, this will be the time to start.

YOUR MATURE WEBSITE: YEAR 6 AND BEYOND

At this stage, you may have 300+ pieces of content on your site. It's time to put on a new hat and start to approach your content like a resource librarian!

You may continue to publish every other week — but there's more you must do. Going forward, focus on directing visitors around your site so they can easily find what they need.

Aim to:

Develop an updating habit. Some of your content is quite old. If it's still being found, is it still reflecting positively on your business? Is it still relevant?

Get a clear view of what content is most popular so you can link back to it *from* newer content and link forward from it *to* newer content. (This simple tip will allow older content to help newer content.)

Master multimedia content and an expanded presence on outside platforms. Make it a habit to repurpose every piece of new content you create, so it's findable in other places and people can discover your website.

CHECKLIST | HOW TO CRAFT VERY IMPORTANT CONTENT

Remember, content marketing that moves you closer to your business goals is *strategic*. That means:

- Keeping your BIG goal front and center
- Looking for keyword phrases that make your content easier to find using search engines
- Aiming to wow your site visitors once they arrive on your page
- Delivering thorough, in-depth content that keeps them engaged, using multimedia to appeal to their senses
- Inviting them to stay connected by featuring either an opt-in incentive or a content upgrade that visitors will share their email addresses to get access to

CHECKLIST | YOUR NEW WEBSITE: BIRTH THROUGH YEAR 1

You have a few important goals in the first year of a brand-new website:

- Make educated guesses about your ideal audience member and create content that will attract those people you'd like to work with
- Build your content creator muscles by sticking to a regular publishing schedule
- Begin establishing your core content categories and creating content to build them out

CHECKLIST | YOUR GROWING WEBSITE: YEAR 2 THROUGH YEAR 5

You'll come into your own as a content creator during these important growth years. This is a time when you establish habits and build on them so you step into your role as a powerful content creator who people pay attention to.

- Focus on crafting high-quality content — even if that means publishing less often. Make your content longer and more detailed. Support your main points with data, if needed. Include multimedia elements to help keep people on your page.
- Build content upgrades that complement the information you share and also grow your email list
- Build authority by occasionally publishing content with direct quotes from thought leaders in your industry
- Listen intently to the audience that you're building, so you can adapt your content topics to their needs
- Practice weaving in promotional content, so you can use

your platform to keep the marketing engine of your business running smoothly

- Repurpose the content you create into different types of media that you feature on platforms outside your website

CHECKLIST | YOUR MATURE WEBSITE: YEAR 6 AND BEYOND

At this growth stage, your role will change yet again. You will continue to create content — more easily now because you have a lot of practice! But because you've developed a large body of content, you will take on the roles of guide to and caretaker of the content you've created.

- Continue publishing Very Important Content every two weeks, and now add organization and quarterly maintenance to your regular tasks
- Use your content categories to display collections of content in a navigation menu, a sidebar, or within your site's footer
- Clarify the current purpose of your site and consider changing the focus of older pieces if they don't reflect your current direction
- Use site analytics data to pinpoint popular pieces for maintenance and repurposing
- Maintain and update existing content with improved headlines, better (and more) images, new information, and updated approaches
- Consider repurposing the ideas in different formats: slide decks, video, checklists, etc.
- Extend a hand to those starting out — become a thought leader by leading

CHECKLIST | THE BODY OF WORK APPROACH TO CONTENT CREATION

Like any creative product, content develops best when it's given the right environment and a combination of time and space to grow into what it's meant to be.

- Approach content creation as a series of small tasks
- Don't put too much pressure to perform on a single piece of content — remember you are building a body of work, not a single masterpiece
- Become aware of the way your environment makes content creation easier or more difficult, and set yourself up to create content when and where you feel most supported

CHECKLIST | THE 4-DAY CONTENT CREATION SYSTEM OR A "LAZY" METHOD FOR CREATING CONTENT

Break up the content creation process over several days. You'll give yourself a chance to see the content more than once, and with fresh eyes that are able to spot holes, confusing areas, or anything that's unclear.

Day 1: Write your headline and subheads

Day 2: Write your main copy

Day 3: Polish and prepare to publish

Day 4: Publish and promote

CHECKLIST | SERVE YOUR SITE VISITORS WITH TARGETED CONTENT

Your website visitors arrive on your site with different levels of awareness about your topic. These levels of awareness reflect their readiness to do business with you! As a content creator, you want to be sure to serve everyone, no matter what stage they're in.

- Beginners have lots of basic questions, so create content that answers "What is __?" and "Why is __ important?" queries
- Intermediate audience members want to begin applying your topic to their lives, so create content that answers their "How do I do __?" questions
- Advanced audience members want high-level information. Create content that answers questions like, "How can I profit from __?" and "How can I boost the results I get from __?"
- The exact amount of content you create for each of these groups will vary depending on your current business goals and the audience you are trying to attract.

CHECKLIST | FIT PROMOTIONS INTO YOUR CONTENT STRATEGY

The core recommendation in this chapter is to look ahead on your calendar, map out what you plan to promote, and then build content that naturally leads people toward appreciating the solution you're going to offer them, but without alienating audience members who aren't interested in the offer.

- Consider creating an email interest list of people who raise their hands (and furnish their email addresses) to find out more about your upcoming offer

- Create a special price or "first dibs" offer just for your interest list
- To entice people to join the email interest list, create in-depth content on the topic your upcoming offer is about and offer it in exchange for adding their email address to the list
- Create purposeful content in the lead-up to your launch — see the example in this chapter for how to do this over a 6-week pre-launch period
- In the lead-up to your offer, weave together content that meets common objections, offers how-to information, and generally builds enthusiasm for the solution you'll offer.

CHECKLIST | REPURPOSING CONTENT FOR FUN, PROFIT & TRAFFIC

Repurposing content means giving your information new life (and additional attention) by transforming it into a different format from its original. As you become a more confident content creator, mastering content repurposing is a natural next step in your development.

- Repurposing is easier when your content uses an underlying structure like the one taught in the Content Marketing Crash Course part of this book, and it's covered in detail in *Master Content Marketing*
- Aim to explore one or two content repurposing techniques at a time
- Start with your most-used content format and use the ideas here to select a way you'll change it into a fresh, new format
- Base your new format selection — and its platform — on what you believe will appeal to the ideal customer you want to reach

- Make content visual, make it move, make it digestible, make it easy to find, and keep promoting it over time

CHECKLIST | BUILD A CONTENT AMPLIFICATION STRATEGY

In a world of content shock, our content amplification efforts are every bit as important as our content creation efforts. Be strategic about how you'll promote the content you work so hard to build.

- Build domain authority with smart, consistent content creation
- Don't live by vanity metrics like social shares — instead, pay attention to the business results delivered by your content
- Share your content on social media, via email, and — for extra special content — with industry thought leaders
- Consider paying to promote your strategically important content
- Use content repurposing as an amplification strategy

CHECKLIST | CONTENT UPGRADES AS EMAIL LIST BUILDERS

Content upgrades are a reliable way to identify people in your audience who are especially interested in a topic you plan to make an offer around. The upgrade expands on the content you're creating with more in-depth information that you offer in exchange for their email address.

- Before creating the upgrade, spend some time thinking about the qualities you're looking for in the ideal customer you want to attract to your offer

- Create a content upgrade that will naturally attract this kind of person
- Less is more! Make a content upgrade that delivers quick results and is easy for you to create
- Embed the opt-in form in your content and use your email marketing program to move these subscribers to a specific list, or tag them with a specific term, so you can remember what they voted an interest in

CHECKLIST | PLAN YEARLY, QUARTERLY, AND MONTHLY CONTENT

Your content plan will grow, change, and evolve as time goes by. Think about your big goals, map out how you'll reach them, and make specific plans that guide your day-to-day work.

- Create a **Yearly Content Plan** that's a broad overview of your business goals and includes a vision for the year ahead
- Map out a **Quarterly Content Plan** that adds dates for promotions and holidays, and work your content around those
- Make a **Monthly Content Plan** that you'll use to guide your week-by-week content creation.

CHECKLIST | MAKING YOUR CONTENT STRATEGY REAL

Committing your content strategy to a visible format you can easily follow means you can avoid sitting in front of your screen wondering what content you need to create this week. Make your plan, and work that plan!

- Commit your content strategy to a format that feels comfortable and easy for you

- At a minimum, be sure your content strategy includes your publishing frequency, content topics, and publishing dates
- Weave in promotional plans, if you have them, so you can use content during the warm-up and launch periods

ACKNOWLEDGMENTS

To my husband, Jim, who has kept things running smoothly in our lives while I had my nose stuck in my laptop, finishing this book. We are overdue for a vacation!

To my beloved community on BIG Brand System, who inquired about this book, repeatedly told me they were waiting for it, and encouraged me along the way. I so appreciate having a ready audience for the words I write, and I hope you find it was worth the wait.

To Jon Morrow, who didn't blink when I showed up in Austin, took him to dinner, and asked if he'd write the foreword for *Master Content Strategy*. You have always believed in my work from the moment we met, and it means more than you'll ever know.

ABOUT THE AUTHOR

Pamela Wilson has been helping people get their ideas out into the world since 1987. She started her career as a marketing consultant and graphic designer, and she opened the doors to her own business in 1992.

Pamela began her online business, BIGBrandSystem.com, in early 2010. At BIG Brand System, she helps ambitious people build online businesses based on their hard-earned expertise — and without the usual feeling of overwhelm. This happens through free information on the site, plus targeted programs, coaching, and a mastermind group.

Pamela is the author of *Master Content Marketing: A Simple Strategy to Cure the Blank Page Blues and Attract a Profitable Audience,* which is the companion to this book. *Master Content Marketing* helps beginning content creators make high-impact content consistently, even if they're not natural-born writers.

She also wrote *Proceed with Confidence: 25 Quick Ways to Boost Your Business Mojo. Proceed with Confidence* is a quick read that's designed to be consumed over your next lunch hour or coffee break.

Pamela lives in Nashville, Tennessee.